The
LONG ROAD
to
FREEDOM

AN ANTHOLOGY OF BLACK MUSIC

The
Long Road
to
FREEDOM

AN ANTHOLOGY OF BLACK MUSIC

Bass Concerto, Drawing by Charles White

1

THE ROOTS

FEATURES VOCAL CONTRIBUTIONS *from Sorrell Booke,
Betty Clotty, Solomon Gbadegesin Hori, Bessie Jones, Kandia,
Toko Mzobe, Asafoiatse Nettey and Emanuel N'Suba*
GHANA CHOIR: *E.K. Acquaye, Nii Amon Kotey,
Francis A. Boschway, Ernest A. Plange, Henry Noye-Nortey,
Randy Larsen, James Nee-Larty, George Thompson,
Richard Netty, Benny Annum, Gideon Arkorful,
Wentworth Ofuatey-Kodjoe, Yaw Gyebi, Leo Mensah,
Thomas Mensah, Kwabena Brown, George Darkeh,
Joe Welsing and Veronica Otoo* GUINEA CHOIR: *David Nzomo,
Frederick Musyoka, Vincent Mbirika, Francis Getao,
Gideon Kioko, Vitalis Ojwang, Thomas Owuor,
Ruth Ntheketha, Nyaboke Okari and Melen Ojenge*
NIGERIA CHOIR: *Garvin Masseau, Sonny Morgan,
Taiwo Duvall, Robert Whitley, Al Humphrey, Moses Mianns,
Adetunji A. Joda, James Folami, Solomon Ilori,
Adegboyega Ilori, Olatunji Oyefuga, Tundi Ajayi,
Emiko Amoye, Solomon Deji Adeyoyin, Daniel Olusegun,
Simon Jiboku, Jemie Samson, Abby Ekwonna,
Flora Etomi, Oluremi Okediji, Mosunmola Ilori,
Eyo Okodi; Hugh Masekela (S. Africa), Jonas Gwangwa
(S. Africa), Sunku Mofokeng (S. Africa), Doreen Faulkner
(S. Africa), David Chikosi (Rhodesia), Assad Kelada (Egypt),
Nadia Kelada (Egypt), Emanuel N'Suba (Congo),
Sherman Sneed (vocal contractor) (U.S.A.),
Carolin Mandara (Tanganyika), Mariam Ali (Zanzibar)
and Willy Kiwanuka (Uganda)*

SHOUTS AND EARLY SPIRITUALS

FEATURES VOCAL CONTRIBUTIONS *from
Harry Belafonte, Erzalene Jenkins, Bessie Jones,
Nannie McNeil and Valentine Pringle*
CHOIR: *Leroy Brodwith, Jennifer Cathy Brown,
Laurence Cartier, Barbara J. Cobb, Charles Colman,
Joseph Crawford, Paul Douglas Franklin, Doris Galiber,
Fileen Gilbert, J. Hamilton Grandison, Hugh Harrell,
Hilda Harris, Pauline P. Hill, Norma Lee Hooper,
Jean La Guerra, Geraldine Overstreet, Eleanor Rogers,
Irene E. Sherrock, Christine Spencer, Maeretha A. Stewart
and Ruth Gibbs Tyler*

LOUISIANA CREOLE

1. **Tombeau, tombeau** *2:35*
   Collected by H. Oster. Directed, Arranged and
   Conducted by Leonard de Paur
   RECORDED SPRING 1962

2. **Je m'en vais finir mes jours**
   "Madelaine" song *3:51*
   Directed, Arranged and Conducted by
   Leonard de Paur
   RECORDED FALL 1962

3. **Dans un brigatoire** *3:25*
   Directed, Arranged and Conducted by
   Leonard de Paur
   RECORDED SPRING 1962

   Au Place Congo

4. **Pour la belle Layotte** *1:21*
   RECORDING DATE UNKNOWN
   FEATURED VOCALIST: *William "Billy" Eaton*

5. **Fomme la dit, mo malheuré** *3:28*
   Collected by Harry Oster. Directed,
   Arranged and Conducted by Leonard de Paur
   RECORDED FALL 1967

6. **Miche Banjo – bamboula** *2:08*
   Directed, Arranged and Conducted by
   Leonard de Paur
   RECORDED FALL 1967
   FEATURED VOCALIST: *Robert Henson*
   BANJO: *Danny Barker*

SLAVE CHRISTMAS

7. **Good Mornin', Good Mornin' –**
   "John Canoe" processional *2:51*
   Collected, Arranged, and Adapted by
   Gracita F. Faulkner
   RECORDING DATE UNKNOWN
   FEATURED VOCALIST: *J. Hamilton Grandison*

8. **All Roun' de Glory Manger** *1:49*
   Directed, Arranged and Conducted by
   Leonard de Paur
   RECORDED SPRING 1962
   FEATURED VOCALISTS: *Erzalene Jenkins*
   and Joseph Crawford

9. **Mary, What You Call Yo' Baby?** *3:04*
   Directed, Arranged and Conducted by
   Leonard de Paur
   RECORDED SPRING 1962
   FEATURED VOCALIST: *Carrie Lee Suter*

10. **Wonderful Councillor** *2:05*
    Collected, Directed, Arranged and
    Conducted by Leonard de Paur
    RECORDED SPRING 1968
    FEATURED VOCALIST: *Harry Belafonte*

FEATURES VOCAL CONTRIBUTIONS *from Harry Belafonte,*
Joseph Crawford, William Eaton, J. Hamilton Grandison,
Robert Henson, Erzalene Jenkins and Carrie Lee Suter
1962 CHOIR: *Marie M. Clegg, Emelda B. Dugais,*
Gracita F. Faulkner, Ruby M. Lee, Jean Benjamin,
Edmond Hall, Louis J. Williams, Miriam Burton,
Doris Galiber, Giselle Diamond, Pauline P. Hill,
Charles Colman, William Eaton, Robert Henson,
George A. Hill, Eugene Thamon, Millard J. Williams,
Sherman Sneed (vocal contractor) and Howard Roberts
1968 CHOIR: *Leroy Brodwith, Jennifer Cathy Brown,*
Laurence Cartier, Barbara J. Cobb, Doris Galiber,
Hilda Harris, Pauline P. Hill, Norma Lee Hooper,
Jean La Guerra, Geraldine Overstreet, Albertine H. Robinson,
Eleanor Rogers, Irene E. Sherrock, Christine Spencer,
Maeretha A. Stewart and Ruth Gibbs Tyler

THE LONG ROAD TO FREEDOM: UNDERGROUND RAILROAD

11. **Follow the Drinking Gourd** *2:44*
    RECORDED FALL 1962
    FEATURED VOCALIST: *Leon Bibb*

12. **Steal Away to Jesus** *3:28*
    Attributed to Nat Turner. Directed, Arranged
    and Conducted by Leonard de Paur
    RECORDED FALL 1961

13. **There's a Meetin' Here Tonight** *1:51*
    Arranged by Ralph Hunter
    RECORDED FALL 1961
    FEATURED VOCALISTS: *Joseph Crawford and*
    an unidentified male vocalist

14. **Many Thousan' Gone** *3:03*
    Arranged and Adapted by Howard A. Roberts
    and Ralph Hunter
    RECORDED FALL 1961

THE LONG ROAD TO FREEDOM: THE WAR

15. **The Colored Volunteer** *3:29*
    Arranged by Ralph Hunter
    RECORDED SPRING 1968
    FEATURED VOCALIST: *Harry Belafonte*

16. **We Look Like Men of War** *5:34*
    RECORDING DATE UNKNOWN
    FEATURED VOCALISTS: *Earl Baker (possibly),*
    Milt Grayson (possibly)

17. **Song of the First Arkansas Volunteers**
    Glory Hallelujah *4:52*
    Directed, Arranged and Conducted by Leonard de Paur
    RECORDED SPRING 1968
    FEATURED VOCALIST: *Harry Belafonte*

18. **Free at Las'** *1:51*
    RECORDED FALL 1961
    FEATURED VOCALISTS: *Joseph Crawford and*
    an unidentified male vocalist

FEATURES VOCAL CONTRIBUTIONS *from Earl Baker,*
Harry Belafonte, Joseph Crawford, Carol Joy Dawkins,
William Eaton, Milt Grayson, Nannie McNeil, Alfred Miller,
Howard Roberts, Eugene Thamon, Ruth Gibbs Tyler,
Millard Williams CHOIR: *Laurence Cartier, Charles Colman,*
Joseph Crawford, Paul D. Franklin, William A. Glover,
John P. Gonsalves, J. Hamilton Grandison, Hugh Harrell,
Robert Henson, George Hill, Melvin E. Jordan, Lawrence Marshall,
Alfred Miller, Felix A. Morris, Jordan Poropat,
Herbert Scott-Gibson, Sherman Sneed (vocal contractor),
William Stewart, Eugene Thamon, Mervin B. Wallace and
Arthur Williams LARGE MIXED CHORUS: *FIRST TENOR VOICES:*
George Adams, Joseph Crawford, Robert Henson,
Charles Joiner, Howard Roberts, Rodester Timmons and
Clyde Turner; SECOND TENOR VOICES: William Eaton,
Ben Foster, Paul Jackson, John Patton, Arthur Williams and
Ned Wright; BARITONE VOICES: Irving Barnes, Eugene Brige,
Charles Colman, J. Hamilton Grandison, Alonzo Jones,
George Marshall and Sherman Sneed (vocal contractor);
BASS VOICES: Earl Baker, Laurence Cartier, Sidney Greenard,
George Hill, Cullen Maiden, Eugene Thamon and
Millard Williams SOPRANO VOICES: *Carol Joy Dawkins,*
Carlotta Freeman, Bernice Hall, Hilda Harris, Lucia Hawkins,
Juanita King, Joy McLean, June McMechen,
Doris Galiber Robert, Christine Spencer, Maeretha A. Stewart,
Catherine Van Buren and Marie Young; ALTO VOICES:
Gale Gordon, Pauline Phelps, Ruth Reynolds, Albertine Robinson,
Ruth Gibbs Tyler, Barbara Webb and Gloria Wynder
INSTRUMENTALISTS:
Garnett Brown TROMBONE, *Burt Collins* TRUMPET, FLUGELHORN,
Warren Covington TROMBONE, *Raymond Crisara* TRUMPET,
FLUGELHORN, *Elayne Jones* FIELD DRUMS, SNARE DRUMS,
Hubert Laws, Jr. PICCOLO, FLUTE, *Jimmy Owens* TRUMPET,
Harvey Phillips TUBA, *Robert Rosengarden* SNARE DRUMS,
Warren I. Smith BASS DRUMS, *John Swallow* BARITONE HORN,
Joseph Venuto FIELD DRUMS, *Joesph Wilder* TRUMPET, FLUGELHORN

COUNTRY MOODS

1. **Ol' Lady From Brewster – children's song** *1:51*
   Collected by Bessie Jones; Directed, Arranged
   and Conducted by Leonard de Paur
   RECORDED SPRING 1969
   FEATURED VOCALISTS: *Vincent Esposito,*
   Kevin Featherstone, Gregory L. Sneed
   and Children's Chorus

2. **Hallie, Come On! – woman's field holler** *1:11*
   RECORDING DATE UNKNOWN
   FEATURED VOCALIST: *Miriam Burton*

3. **Run Squirrel, Whoa Mule – game song** *1:30*
   RECORDING DATE UNKNOWN
   FEATURED VOCALIST: *Thelma Drayton*

4. **Fox Chase – mouth organ** *3:18*
   RECORDED SUMMER 1970
   FEATURED VOCALISTS: *Sonny Terry and*
   Brownie McGhee

5. **Chickens Done Crowed – sunrise holler** *1:36*
   RECORDED WINTER 1962
   FEATURED VOCALIST: *Valentine Pringle*

6. **'Way Go Lily – children's song** *1:30*
   Collected by Bessie Jones; Adapted, Directed,
   Arranged and Conducted by Leonard de Paur
   RECORDED SPRING 1969
   FEATURED VOCALIST: *Children's Chorus*

7. **Shine On – graveyard holler** *1:41*
   RECORDED WINTER 1962
   FEATURED VOCALIST: *Ned Wright*

8. **Grey Goose – ballad** *2:46*
   RECORDED WINTER 1962
   FEATURED VOCALIST: *Bessie Jones*

9. **Pick a Bale o' Cotton – hoedown** *5:08*
   RECORDED SUMMER 1970
   FEATURED VOCALISTS: *Sonny Terry and*
   Brownie McGhee

10. **Li'l Gal, Li'l Gal – game song** *1:22*
    RECORDED WINTER 1962
    FEATURED VOCALIST: *Bessie Jones*

11. **Go to Sleepy – lullaby** *1:43*
    RECORDING DATE UNKNOWN
    FEATURED VOCALIST: *Harry Belafonte*
    GUITAR: *Al Shackman*

FEATURES VOCAL CONTRIBUTIONS *from*
Harry Belafonte, Miriam Burton, Thelma Drayton,
Chas Featherstone, Ray Franklin, Bessie Jones,
Brownie McGhee, Valentine Pringle, Sonny Terry and Ned Wright
CHILDREN'S CHOIR: *Irene (Escalera) Cara, Melanie Colman,*
Norma Lynn de Paur, Leonard de Paur, Robin L. DeSilva,
Ivan Espinosa, Giancarlo Esposito, Vincent Esposito,
Kevin Featherstone, Lisa Huggins, Gregory L. Sneed,
Darryl Thomas and Sherman Sneed (vocal contractor)

CITY MOODS

12. **I Got 'Em – street cry** *1:54*
    Collected, Directed, Arranged and Conducted
    by Leonard de Paur
    RECORDED SPRING 1968
    FEATURED VOCALIST: *Valentine Pringle*

13. **Hambone, Hambone – children's pattin'** *2:41*
    RECORDED WINTER 1962
    FEATURED VOCALIST: *Tyrone Cooper*

14. **Watermelon Man – blues** *1:21*
    RECORDING DATE UNKNOWN
    FEATURED VOCALIST: *Ned Wright*

15. **Fare Thee Well, Oh Honey – blues** *5:49*
    RECORDED WINTER 1962
    FEATURED VOCALIST: *Gloria Lynne*

16. **Blackberry Woman – street cry** *1:07*
    RECORDED WINTER 1962
    FEATURED VOCALIST: *Lillian Hayman*

17. **Easy Rider Blues – blues** *5:27*
    RECORDED SPRING 1962
    FEATURED VOCALIST: *Joe Williams*
    GUITAR: *Al Shackman*

18. **Oh, Johnny Brown – ring game** *1:51*
    RECORDED WINTER 1962
    FEATURED VOCALIST: *Sharon G. Williams*

19. **I Got 'Em – street cry** *1:13*
    RECORDED WINTER 1962
    FEATURED VOCALIST: *Valentine Pringle*

20. **Black Woman – blues** *4:06*
    RECORDING DATE UNKNOWN
    FEATURED VOCALIST: *Brownie McGhee*

21. **Watermelon Man – street cry** *:44*
    RECORDING DATE UNKNOWN
    FEATURED VOCALIST: *Ned Wright*

FEATURES VOCAL CONTRIBUTIONS *from*
Tyrone Cooper, Lillian Hayman, Gloria Lynne,
Brownie McGhee, Valentine Pringle, Joe Williams,
Sharon G. Williams and Ned Wright

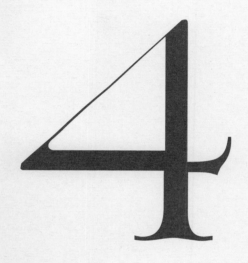

BALLADS AND FROLICS

1. **Let the Deal Go Down** *4:16*
RECORDING DATE UNKNOWN
FEATURED VOCALISTS: *Godfrey Cambridge,*
Joseph Crawford, Brownie McGhee
and unidentified others

2. **Betty and Dupree** *6:44*
RECORDED SPRING 1962
FEATURED VOCALIST: *Joe Williams*
GUITAR: *Brownie McGhee*
PIANO: *Herman Foster*

3. **Eas' Man** *2:53*
RECORDED FALL 1962
FEATURED VOCALIST: *Leon Bibb*

4. **John Henry** *3:27*
POSSIBLE RECORDING DATES: WINTER 1962,
SPRING 1964, SUMMER 1967
FEATURED VOCALIST: *Valentine Pringle*

5. **Boll Weevil** *6:07*
RECORDED SPRING 1968
FEATURED VOCALIST: *Harry Belafonte*
GUITAR: *Al Shackman*

FEATURES VOCAL CONTRIBUTIONS *from*
Harry Belafonte, Leon Bibb, Walter P. Brown,
Godfrey Cambridge, Joseph Crawford,
Robert Henson, Jack Hodges, Brownie McGhee,
Valentine Pringle, Howard Roberts and Joe Williams

BAD MEN, BOOZE AND MINSTRELS

6. **Stagolee** *5:42*
Collected, Directed, Arranged and
Conducted by Leonard de Paur
RECORDED SPRING 1971
FEATURED VOCALIST: *Cortez Franklin*
GUITAR: *Lennie Pogan*

7. **Joe Turner Blues** *4:12*
RECORDED WINTER 1962
FEATURED VOCALIST: *Gloria Lynne*
PIANO: *Herman Foster*

8. **Honey, Take a Whiff on Me** *3:39*
Collected and Adapted by Leonard de Paur
and Benjamin Carter. Directed, Arranged
and Conducted by Leonard de Paur
RECORDED SPRING 1971
FEATURED VOCALIST: *Ben Carter*
GUITAR: *Lennie Pogan*

Folk-Minstrel Scene

9. **Go 'Long Muley** *3:35*
Text collected from folklore.
Tune by Leonard de Paur
RECORDED WINTER 1971

10. **My Baby in a Guinea Blue Gown** *4:40*
Directed, Arranged and Conducted by
Leonard de Paur
RECORDED WINTER 1971

11. **Dat Liar** *6:52*
Text and tune Collected and Adapted by
Leonard de Paur
RECORDED WINTER 1971
FEATURED VOCALIST: *Milton Grayson*

12. **Finale** *:45*

FEATURES VOCAL CONTRIBUTIONS *from*
Harry Belafonte, Ben Carter, Charles Colman, Cortez Franklin,
Milton Grayson, Robert Henson, Gloria Lynne,
Larry Marshall, Gregory L. Sneed and Sherman Sneed

MUSCLES AND SWEAT

1. **Ho Boys, Cancha Line 'Em?** *2:56*
   RECORDED WINTER 1962
   FEATURED VOCALIST: *Valentine Pringle*

2. **Good Ir'n** *6:03*
   *Collected and Arranged by Leonard de Paur
   and Harry Belafonte*
   RECORDED SPRING 1968
   FEATURED VOCALIST: *Harry Belafonte*

3. **Go On, Ol' Gator** *3:00*
   RECORDING DATE UNKNOWN

4. **Doncha Hear Yo' Po' Mother Callin'?** *3:42*
   RECORDING DATE UNKNOWN

5. **River Sounding Chant** *3:17*
   POSSIBLE RECORDING DATES:
   WINTER 1962, SPRING 1967
   FEATURED VOCALISTS: *Charles Colman and
   William Eaton*

6. **Nobody's Business, Lord, but Mine** *4:24*
   *Collected and Arranged by Leonard de Paur
   and Harry Belafonte*
   RECORDED SPRING 1968
   FEATURED VOCALIST: *Harry Belafonte*

FEATURES VOCAL CONTRIBUTIONS *from
Harry Belafonte, Charles Colman, William Eaton,
Leonard Etienne, Bernice Hall and Valentine Pringle*
CHOIR: *Leroy Brodwith, Laurence Cartier, Charles Colman,
Joseph Crawford, Paul D. Franklin, William A. Glover,
John P. Gonsalves, Marvin Goodis, J. Hamilton Grandison,
Hugh Harrell, Robert Henson, Lawrence Marshall,
Alfred Miller, Jordan Poropat, Earl Rogers, Herbert Scott-Gibson,
Cal Sexton, Sherman Sneed (vocal contractor),
William Stewart, Eugene Thamon, Marvin B. Wallace
and Arthur Williams*

MY GOD IS A ROCK

7. **My God Is a Rock** *3:03*
   Collected and Arranged by Leonard de Paur
   RECORDED SPRING 1968
   FEATURED VOCALIST: *Harry Belafonte*

8. **We Are Climbin' Jacob's Ladder** *2:44*
   RECORDING DATE UNKNOWN

9. **I Am So Glad** *2:28*
   *Collected, Directed, Arranged and Conducted
   by Leonard de Paur*
   RECORDED SPRING 1968
   FEATURED VOCALIST: *Harry Belafonte*

10. **I'll Never Turn Back No Mo' –
    and excerpt from Dr. King speech** *6:11*
    Arranged by Hal Johnson
    RECORDED WINTER 1961
    FEATURED VOCALIST: *Irving Barnes*
    SPEAKER: *Dr. Martin Luther King, Jr.*
    DATE OF SPEECH UNKNOWN
    LISCENSE GRANTED BY IPM, ATLANTA, GEORGIA, AS
    MANAGER OF THE ESTATE OF MARTIN LUTHER KING, JR.

11. **Lord, I Don't Feel Noways Tired** *2:35*
    Arranged by Hal Johnson
    RECORDED WINTER 1961
    FEATURED VOCALIST: *Howard Roberts*

FEATURES VOCAL CONTRIBUTIONS *from Irving Barnes,
Harry Belafonte, Dr. Martin Luther King, Jr., Howard Roberts*
CHOIR: *Ernest Barnard Alexander, Leroy Brodwith,
Jennifer Cathy Brown, Mary Ellen Brown, Laurence Cartier,
Barbara J. Cobb, Charles Colman, Mary Elizabeth Cook,
Joseph Crawford, Paul Douglas Franklin, Doris Galiber,
Eileen Gilbert, J. Hamilton Grandison, Hugh Harrell,
Hilda Harris, Robert Henson, George Hill, Pauline P. Hill,
Norma Lee Hooper, Erzalene Jenkins, Jean La Guerra,
Laurence Marshall, Nannie McNeil, Alfred Miller,
Jessie Pearl Miller, Asalee L. Mitchell, Felix A. Morris, Jr.
Geraldine Overstreet, Jordan Poropat, Andrea Pamela Putter,
Albertine H. Robinson, Eleanor Rogers, Herbert Scott-Gibson,
Irene E. Sherrock, Sherman Sneed, Christine Spencer,
Maeretha A. Stewart, Carrie Lee Suter, Laura Ann Taylor,
Eugene Thamon, Ruth Gibbs Tyler, Fredericks Washington,
Mervin Bertel Wallace and Arthur Williams*
TRACKS 10 AND 11 *feature the* LARGE MIXED CHORUS:
*FIRST TENOR VOICES: George Adams, Joesph Crawford,
Robert Henson, Charles Joiner, Howard Roberts,
Rodester Timmons and Clyde Turner; SECOND TENOR VOICES:
William Eaton, Ben Foster, Paul Jackson, John Patton,
Arthur Williams and Ned Wright; BARITONE VOICES:
Irving Barnes, Eugene Brige, Charles Colman,
J. Hamilton Grandison, Alonzo Jones, George Marshall and
Sherman Sneed (vocal contractor); BASS VOICES: Earl Baker,
Laurence Cartier, Sidney Greenard, George Hill,
Cullen Maiden, Eugene Thamon and Millard Williams;
SOPRANO VOICES: Carol Joy Dawkins, Carlotta Freeman,
Bernice Hall, Hilda Harris, Lucia Hawkins, Juanita King,
Joy McLean, June McMechen, Doris Galiber Robert,
Christine Spencer, Maeretha A. Stewart, Marie Young,
Catherine Van Buren; ALTO VOICES: Gale Gordon,
Pauline Phelps, Ruth Reynolds, Albertine Robinson,
Ruth Gibbs Tyler, Barbara Webb and Gloria Wynder*

**THE LONG ROAD TO FREEDOM: AN ANTHOLOGY OF BLACK MUSIC
FEATURES MUSICAL CONTRIBUTIONS FROM:**
GUITARS: *Ernie Calabria, Brownie McGhee,
Walter Raim and Al Shackman* BANJO: *Danny Barker*
PIANO: *Herman Foster* FIDDLES: *Rupert Moore and
Ray Nance* PERCUSSION: *Danny Barrajanos,
Ralph MacDonald and Mossi Mians* HARMONICA:
Sonny Terry PENNY WHISTLE: *Herbert Levy*
WASHTUB BASS: *Bob Harris*
All tracks published by Clara Music Publishing Corp. (ASCAP) except as noted.

BONUS
DVD

**Footsteps on *The Long Road to Freedom:
The Making of the Anthology of Black Music***

Harry Belafonte, the producers and archivists discuss
the genesis of the project and its relevance today as
well as provide details on the discovery and restoration
of this musically rich masterpiece.

Among the Special Features found on this DVD
are Harry Belafonte's reminiscence of that special
period, filmed at the original recording hall in
NYC, Webster Hall, the reaction to the discovery
of this long-lost treasure, biographies of key
participants and musicians, Web site links, a
message from the National Underground
Railroad Freedom Center and much more.

A MUSICAL HISTORY OF AMERICA'S AFRICANS

The songs of Black America sung by artists inspired by its struggle

BY HARRY BELAFONTE

WHEN I WAS A YOUNGSTER, RADIO AND CINEMA WERE THE GREAT PASTIMES AND DOMINATED MOST OF THE CULTURE THAT COMMANDED ATTENTION. THE MENU OF OFFERINGS FOR AFRICAN AMERICANS WAS, HOWEVER, MORE OFTEN THAN NOT, DEGRADING AND HUMILIATING. SUCH WAS A SHOW THAT RADIO GAVE US CALLED "AMOS AND ANDY"—A COMEDY SHOW SO SKILLFULLY WRITTEN AND PERFORMED THAT FEW HOMES IN WHITE OR BLACK AMERICA WERE NOT TOUCHED BY IT.

Not many cultural offerings, even to this day, have ever equaled its public favor. In cinema, film after film constantly depicted Africans and their American slave descendants as a subhuman species.

In my early childhood living in Harlem, I remember my mother once hauled us off to see a movie called *Tarzan of the Apes*. The film's depiction of Africa and its people gave me my earliest impression of Africans. It painted

J'Accuse #9, Drawing by Charles White

a landscape of a dark and evil continent inhabited by savage natives, whose only hope for a place in the civilized world was through the kindness and courage of the white Adonis who swung from tree to tree. D. W. Griffith's vehemently racist 1915 film, *Birth of a Nation*, an epic saga of the American Civil War, was perhaps the cruelest blow of all. Its overwhelming popularity set the tone for how Black citizens were to be perceived for the rest of the 20th century. These distortions by popular culture fueled the cruelest myths about race, provoking extreme social violence, and resulting in the lynching of Black citizens and the burning down of their communities.

Were it not for the songs and folk stories of the African oral tradition, much that tells us about who we are would be unknown. Every song in this collection speaks to the experience of the journey that captives from Africa have had to endure on the long road to freedom.

In the beginning, our music was our source of hope, our well of truth. With the power and resources of white society directed at perpetuating the myth of our inferiority, we were in a constant struggle for truth about our heritage. Having no access to printing presses or centers of learning, we used music as a link to our history and as documentation of our social and political experiences.

At the turn of the 20th century, the invention of the phonograph ensured that music could be stored and retrieved. But like all technology, it served the tastes of those who controlled it; consequently, much of what was and is of value is missing. With all the music that has emerged from Black America, there are large volumes of treasures yet to be uncovered.

Although the depression of the 1930s was a time of much suffering, it was also a time of great reward. Through the federal subsidy of the arts, America experienced its greatest cultural renaissance. The WPA (Works Project Administration) subsidized artists in every discipline and unfolded a richness of artistic expression yet unparalleled.

The literary world produced such luminaries as John Steinbeck, Richard Wright, Ernest Hemingway, William Faulkner, Eugene O'Neill, Langston Hughes and F. Scott Fitzgerald; the world of dance gave us Martha Graham and Katherine Dunham; the theater yielded Orson Wells, Paul Robeson, Uta Hagen and The Group Theater, with Elia Kazan, John Garfield, Clifford Odets, Stella and Luther Adler; painters like Charles White, Romar Bearden, Jackson Pollock, and Jacob Lawrence emerged, as did musicians and singers, including Nobel Sissle, Woody Guthrie, Big Bill Brunzy, Bessie Smith and many others.

Tapping into this cultural treasure chest inspired us to create a large part of what is contained in these recordings. How fortunate we are that so many of America's hidden musical treasures are now housed in the Library of Congress. Through the government's sponsorship, documentarians, going into the most rural parts of the country wherever there was a voice to be heard or an instrument to be played, recorded them. Within this archive exist many of the richest expressions of Black culture.

It was during one of these missions that Huddie Ledbetter, more popularly known as "Leadbelly," was discovered while serving sentence on a chain gang for manslaughter. So compelling were his songs that, on two occasions, he was pardoned.

Songs from the slave plantations retained their authenticity in the prisons of the American South. Men serving time on the chain gang under inhumane conditions called upon experiences handed down from the earliest days of slavery in order to survive their prison journey. Leonard de Paur studied the prison culture and, along with material

J'Accuse #1, Drawing by Charles White

gathered from the Library of Congress, brought to life the stunning choral works heard in this collection. Mr. de Paur petitioned for access to chain-gang prisoners but was denied. In one rejection, prison officials criticized him for trying to "glorify criminality." Considering that these prison sources had been previously accessed by white researchers, Mr. de Paur could not dismiss the belief that his rejection was based upon race.

Of the many musical forms that have emerged from Black culture, the most underserved is the choral art form best exemplified by the sacred song traditions as sung by the Fisk Jubilee Singers in the last half of the 19th century. By the beginning of the 20th century, Black colleges throughout the South followed suit and gave stimulus to this form. And the music flourished. The achievements of Hall Johnson and Leonard de Paur, in formally notating and composing the spiritual and folk songs of African America, ensured that choirs the world over will always have the opportunity to sing the songs that tell the story of our history.

Christianity was no small player in the evolution of slavery. The church's participation in the trafficking of human beings became the moral justification for holding millions of Africans in bondage for over two centuries. For reasons that were not all moral, the same religion would later find it necessary to work for the abolition of slavery. However, by this time slaves were well immersed in the practice of Christianity.

When first brought to this continent, Africans were enjoined from speaking. Slave owners feared their slaves and the constant threat of rebellion. Punishment of extreme cruelty was often invoked for the smallest of offenses. Disagreeing with one's master, challenging his authority or plotting an escape was punishable by whippings, removal of one's tongue or genitalia, and frequently death.

Slaves were not allowed to converse with one another until they learned the tongue of their masters. The church became their tutor. White "slave preachers," teaching the language of the master through the teachings of the Bible, were hired to travel from plantation to plantation to instruct their captive students. The church was the center for all social gatherings. It became the place where the slave could speak, sing and trade stories, albeit under the watchful eye of the master or his representatives. The content of early Black music was predominantly religious.

"The Sermon" (on Disc 1), in *The Slave Catechism*, which defined Christian expectations of them, was an oppressive document. One of the most popular hymns, "Amazing Grace," sung in the context of this edict, puts much in perspective about the psychological conditioning of slaves.

Many songs of the church became the instruments through which much early history was documented and passed on. Every grouping of words in what appeared to be simple hymns was filled with symbols of hope and aspiration for freedom and dignity. These songs became the underground language. Each had a story to tell. Each was rooted in an experience of human degradation that was central to the creation of a culture that set the African American apart from others.

The systematic genocide practiced against Native Americans stands as testimony in defining the extent to which Europeans were prepared to go in their hegemonic conquest. Both the extermination of Native Americans and the enslavement of Africans were justified as necessary for the taming of "heathens" and the protection of "higher civilization." America's reluctance to recognize its full measure of responsibility in the creation and shaping of these inhumane ventures has severely inhibited its ability to

J'Accuse #2, *Drawing by Charles White*

J'Accuse #3, Drawing by Charles White

find peace. This resistance, however, factors in the shaping of its culture. In the 19th century, nothing illustrated this fact more vividly than the art of minstrelsy. This medieval European art form, finding its way into the slave populace, took on a distinctly heightened presence in American culture. Unlike its European antecedent, it became more than song: The Negro minstrel show became a highly developed theatre piece. From a large, richly costumed cast of players, Negroes sang songs, told jokes, did impersonations and danced intricately choreographed steps that captured everyone's fancy. White performers, attracted to the magnificence of what they saw, immediately co-opted the style. Donned with blackface from burnt cork, large exaggerated lips painted white, and with movements of broad clown buffoonery, they mimicked their Black counterparts. Overwhelmingly successful, it became the rage of popular culture, ensuring that it would never be the same again for the Black performers. To make a living, Black minstrels were forced to reinvent themselves, and did so by adapting the demeaning characteristics created by their white plagiarists. The image of the lazy, shiftless buffoon would be our burden for almost a century. Many songs of the day, some written by popular songwriter Stephen Foster about "the darkies," perpetuated this curse.

In my lifetime, Americans of African descent have been called Colored, Negro, Black and, most recently, African American. A lifetime spent in search of title. No other group has suffered this dilemma, no other group has had our experience. To be systematically denied a relationship to and an understanding of the past, and to be forced to live an existence as second-class citizens have forever left us in conflict with society. It has always been of great wonderment to me how, in our quest for identity, Black Americans have so often alluded to our Africanness, yet, despite our proclamations,

Black people know little about Africa or the history of our journey. White America knows even less. This absence of knowledge of our history greatly impedes our ability to complete the journey to our liberation. It also diminishes our democracy. Hearing the songs contained in this volume and the thousands of others like them, and understanding the history from where they have come go a long way in helping us to learn the greater truth.

In 1954, when this project began, segregation was still legal in America, and most African countries were far from independence. These conditions greatly impeded our ability to access the sources of music contained herein. Recording this work in an acoustically controlled environment was a key objective. When we started this project, stereo was in its infancy and, although it would have been most desirable to record at the site of origin, the costs were prohibitive and the mobile units of the day were not yet sophisticated enough to go traipsing all over the country.

So we brought the country to New York. Webster Hall was to be our home for seven years and the engineers at RCA took great pride and delight in recording this wide range of musical sounds and effects on the new element of the day called tape.

The journey in producing this work has been as varied as it has been challenging. Our mission to bring together this unique cast of musical artists from various regions of the United States and Africa to tell this American story was not without its unusual and difficult moments.

How fortunate we were to have had Bessie Jones, a woman of remarkable talent with an overwhelming passion for the songs of her culture, in our midst. Living in the Georgia Sea Islands, untouched by 20th-century industrial development, and existing under conditions not too distant from those of their slave ancestors, the citizens of her community still sang songs and hymns of slavery. The field hollers, the children's game songs, the blues, the church songs of slavery, which still remain true to their original form and content, have graced this anthology. Bessie Jones wanted to come to New York but would do no flying. So it was for all her group. In looking at the budget, it was the only time I wished I owned a bus company! Sonny Terry and Brownie McGhee, known for their constant feuding, were, for the umpteenth time, not speaking to one another, but nonetheless performed some of their most wonderful work together for this recording. One night, in my backstage dressing room at the Riviera Hotel in Las Vegas, Joe Williams, whose great love of singing folk music was known to but a few, for the first time met Brownie McGhee. In the wee hours of the morning, while we sipped our favorite mixes, they began swapping stories and songs, which culminated in this recording of their only performance together. Young Valentine Pringle had a voice like no other, but hearing the magnificence of the choir during rehearsals made him fearful because he didn't read music. He at first resisted our invitation to come on board until he heard that I didn't read music either. All of these artists, with their great diversity of sounds, along with the musical threads that make up this quilt of history, are testimony to its importance and beauty.

Charles White's portrait of Leadbelly, *Goodnight Irene*, is the cover of this anthology. White was a longtime friend, and the many experiences we shared gave special meaning to our relationship. His paintings inspired me, moved me deeply and gave me strength and clarity of purpose. In troubled times, he inspired courage. From his own experiences, he found empathy and identity with the objectives of this anthology. White came to many of the sessions, listened as the work unfolded, and gave of himself and his art.

This work would not exist had it not been for the commitment and support of George Marek. Forty years ago, as head of RCA's vast recording company, he authorized the making of this anthology. As a Jew of Austrian birth and having fled the horrors of Nazi conquest, he was able to empathize and bring a shared sense of history to our project. Where some in his employ suggested they sensed little bottom line value, he made it abundantly clear that his commitment to the fulfillment of our objectives was absolute. He came to almost every session and delighted in all that he heard. The sessions covering the African songs sung by students, some of whom came from Ghana and Nigeria just for the recording, were of particular meaning to him. On the evening of one especially difficult day, as we had dinner at his home, George's wife, Muriel, sensing our emotional drain, suggested we take a break from the project to regain our clarity. The following week, George, Muriel, my family and I found ourselves in the midst of a most remarkable group of drummers from the region of Kankan, in the heart of Guinea in West Africa. Some of these drummers are heard on the first CD under "Roots."

We are forever grateful to all who participated in this project. Our colleagues Leonard de Paur, George Marek, Sonny Terry, Brownie McGhee, Joe Williams, Valentine Pringle, Ned Wright, Bobby Henson, Sherman Sneed, Dr. Martin Luther King, Jr., and others are no longer with us. How fortunate for us that we can be the beneficiaries of their contributions!

Thank you, Alex Miller, for your insight, your passion and your commitment in seeing this through its final passage. You and your colleagues have been indispensable.

Thank you, Buddha-BMG for, in times like these, making *The Long Road to Freedom* your priority. What a journey, what a time!!

As for myself ... I'm just blessed.

THE FOLLOWING ARE EDITED EXCERPTS OF AN INTERVIEW WITH HARRY BELAFONTE REGARDING THE CREATION OF *THE LONG ROAD TO FREEDOM: AN ANTHOLOGY OF BLACK MUSIC* AS TOLD TO ALEX MILLER, HEAD OF BUDDHA RECORDS. THE INTERVIEW WAS CONDUCTED AT WEBSTER HALL, THE SITE OF THE ORIGINAL RECORDINGS, ON JUNE 21, 2000.

As a young child of West Indian parents growing up in Harlem, I remember how filled I was with wonderment about the great diversity that sat within the Black community there. Not only was there a West Indian community that gave much to the causes of the Caribbean, but also, a few blocks from where I lived, I could hear Cubans all day long playing Latin music. I could also hear the folks from the English-speaking Caribbean playing the music of the lower Caribbean. Not too far from where we were living, I could hear the voices coming out of the churches of the community, which were made up mostly of African Americans from the South.

"I DECIDED THAT, AS ROBESON SAID,
THE PURPOSE OF ART IS NOT JUST TO
SHOW LIFE AS IT IS, BUT ALSO TO
SHOW LIFE AS IT SHOULD BE."

Harlem itself was a community just filled with music everywhere we went. The Apollo Theater housed the great orchestras and the great popular artists of the day, who brought the influences of jazz along with the nuances and dimensions of popular culture from around America that were rooted in the Black experience. We really had quite a remarkable environment.

As I grew up and looked at the world beyond Harlem, I was quite fascinated by how little America knew about the culture of its Black citizens. In New York's Harlem, in Chicago and in New Orleans, you could see a microcosm of all that was Black America in these major cities. It wasn't until you entered into rural Black America that you began to discover a whole other nuance, a whole other style, another way in which people spoke to their lives, their interests. So much of the history of Black America is rooted in the mountains, in the hills, in the valleys of rural America.

How little we knew of all of this. How little we knew of each other, even within our own groupings. When I came to understand this, I felt that, somehow, I would like to be able to bring together all of the nuances that made up Black life musically, and deliver it as a work that might bring people not only pleasure and joy, but also instruction. This would give everyone—Black Americans, white Americans, people globally—an opportunity to know how truly multidimensional the Black citizens of this country really are, and how diverse as well as how specific our history is.

I decided that, as Robeson said, the purpose of art is not just to show life as it is, but also to show life as it should be. And in this context, I found that folk art does exactly that. It not only records life as life is being experienced, but much of the music—especially the music being written by Leadbelly, and music written by people like Woody Guthrie and others—is filled with hope, with inspiration and the promise of a greater and a brighter tomorrow.

A representative from RCA who went to the Village Vanguard to see me perform began the earliest of negotiations in order to have me sign with the label; I did. And my very early works were received not only with critical support and some acclaim, but I was quite astounded at the fact that the music I was singing, which in no way reflected anything that even closely resembled the pop art of the day, had worked its way to the attention of disc jockeys and to those who would play the music that I so enthusiastically wanted to perform. This was, for me, a great curiosity, and for RCA it was a great promise of things to come.

I stayed rooted to the folk culture and toured across the length and breadth of America. I began to go mostly into the universities to perform. And I found, in the universities, a huge constituency of my peers, other young people who expressed great delight in the music that I was bringing to them. In this context, I began to learn more about this country, more about its hurts and more about its pleasures, more about its oppression and more about its great and feisty need for its own liberation.

I suggested to RCA that we attempt to create a work that reflected the folk culture of the place where I grew up as a young boy—the Caribbean, particularly the island of Jamaica. This was the home of my mother and my father, and where so many of my relatives still lived and worked on plantations.

The idea struck the A&R reps and certain forces within RCA as a very silly concept. America, which was in many ways so very closed to its own interests, did not have much appetite for that which was not American. That which came from other parts of the world found very little resonance at the center of American pop culture, so that, although as a diverse nation we're made up of so many different cultures and so many different nationalities, we ourselves as a people have very limited appreciation for the cultures of Europe, the cultures of Asia, and certainly the cultures of Africa.

Having been resisted somewhat aggressively by the powers that be, I one day had occasion to have dinner with the head of RCA, a man by the name of George Marek, who originally came from Austria. He was a remarkable human being, musician and musicologist, a man who was deeply rooted in the history of music and, as a matter of fact, had written several books on Beethoven, Brahms and Schubert. He was very well-versed and highly intelligent—very much the intellectual—and was deeply committed to music and to culture.

At this dinner, I expressed to him my sense of loss that there was not more encouragement for this album of music from the Caribbean. He listened to my thoughts on the subject, and two days after this dinner, I got a call from RCA suggesting to me that there was now favor somewhere within the organization for this album. Obviously, George Marek had heard my tale of woe, had intervened and, with his power, had gotten me into the studio to record this album, which was ultimately titled *Calypso*.

Much about that now is pretty much history. The album took off and, if the Academy of Recording Arts and Sciences is correct in the story they tell, and if *Billboard* is correct in the stories they have told, it became the first LP in the history of the record business to, within one year, sell a million copies.

This, of course, not only stimulated the record industry in general, but it certainly delighted RCA to no end. And they decided that they would begin to move resources behind me as fully as they possibly could. George Marek became my mentor.

"...AMERICA WAS EXPRESSING ITS VULNERABILITY, ITS OPENNESS, ITS WILLINGNESS TO HEAR THE MUSIC OF OTHER CULTURES..."

Although the record industry found great delight in this economic fallout and in the great richness that was coming out of this world, what I really took delight in was that America was expressing its vulnerability, its openness, its willingness to hear the music of other cultures, and that whoever had defined America as a closed society unwilling to hear the voice of others or the culture of other people—well, here was an example of a rejection of that concept and that theory.

I was encouraged, then, to not only bring forth more of this music, but to go to other places. I began to sing songs in other languages. I began to dig more deeply into Africa for the richness that came out of that culture, out of that continent. And I began to look more deeply into the music of rural Black America. Of course, for me, rural Black America was almost like another culture—a place that was foreign, certainly to the American pop experience.

As I travelled into the world of the Georgia Sea Islands; as I delved deeply into the music of Leadbelly and the chain-gang experience of Black Americans; as I entered into the heart of the labor movement and went into the mines of Appalachia in West Virginia; and as I heard what the miners had to say—miners whose music came from Ireland, from Wales, even from Germany—the richness that came out of these cultures began to bathe me so fully, that I was very heady with the joy of it all. One day, I went to George Marek and told him that, if the album of the music of the Caribbean was any example of what was out in the world at large for us, then we should take a good, hard look at the root music of Black America.

We should be able to prepare this music and put it together in a way that would not only delight those who would hear it, but also in a way that would instruct and stimulate the listener with its history and the remarkable poetry that came out of this art. I played samples of it for George and he instantly understood and began to relish the discovery for himself. He took a personal interest in trying to put this music in an environment that not only sustained the mission, but brought to it as much access to the public at large as it could possibly have.

Once I came to understand the enormity of the gift that George Marek was bringing to the situation in getting this project launched, and when I examined the potential of what it could do, I was really overwhelmed.

I felt it incumbent upon me to ensure that the integrity of the work would in no way be violated. But since nothing like this had ever been attempted before, there was great question as to the approach. At first, the idea was to take a mobile unit to the various places in the South in order to get to this culture. However, upon examination and analysis, we concluded that it would be much easier to bring the artists to the technology than to have the technology go out and try to find the artists.

The next step was to find the voices that most authenticated the music. It was also necessary to find those who were gifted and who had the art and the creative power to translate the music, so that they could bring their gifts to the table and help yield the results we were trying to achieve. George Marek felt that we should commit ourselves to finding the best in Black America who could document and authenticate the material.

Certainly, the richness of Black music and Black culture is to be found in the group context. Most of the power that comes out of Black music comes out of the church. Much of it came out of environments in which large groups of people were constantly being thrown together. If it wasn't for the purpose of worship, then it was for the purpose of work and labor. So, the music that Black people sang in the fields when they worked and the music that they sang in the churches they attended was very rich with expressions of Black hope and aspiration. And certainly, where Black suffering was to be seen in its extreme—the prisons of America, the chain gangs of America, where men were sent out to do cruel and inhumane work—what helped them get through that oppression, through the day of toil, were the songs that they sang.

And in this music—whether it was in the church, in the fields, harvesting cotton, getting taters and chopping everything they could chop—was also the history of the pain and the hopes, filled with metaphor, filled with subtextual information. What people heard on the surface was only the surface. When you dug deeper into the material, in almost every instance you would find something being stated that was connected to Black hopes for a better day, for a better life, for freedom—freedom to love, freedom to worship, freedom to embrace, freedom to choose a life that was more rewarding than the ones that were being experienced.

It came in many forms: It came in the blues; it came in the game songs that children sang; it came in the lonely songs women sang, wishing that life could be better for them, their children and their men; and it came in the music of the church.

We felt that we had to call upon the greatest musicologist of the day to not only define this music, but to put it together in ways that carried with it great artistic integrity, while reflecting the integrity of the source from which all of this music came. One of the greatest such voices of the day was that of a man by the name of Hall Johnson, who was revered through the musical communities of the world for his tremendous capacity to draw from and write about the richness of Black life. Not only was the Hall Johnson Choir most revered, but of extreme importance and benefit to all was the fact that Hall Johnson wrote to capture the music and to put it permanently into the libraries of the world.

He and a young protégé of his named Leonard de Paur are the two most powerful forces on the musical scene to have come out of Black culture. They possessed the intellectual, as well as the artistic capacity to notate this music on paper, while closely preserving the sounds of its origin. They refined it somewhat, and brought their nuances to it, but there was no question that the great integrity of the work was being protected.

Leonard de Paur auditioned and hand-picked the greatest voices from all over the country, who came to make up the most powerful choral ensemble that could be found in America.

The soloists were picked not only for their musical power and gift, but also for their individual voices, some of which were touched with a very unique print and identity, so that each soloist brought a singular

experience to what audiences would hear, backed up by a rich vocal ensemble.

Certainly there were no greater folk artists in the universe than Sonny Terry and Brownie McGhee. This remarkable man—Brownie McGhee—who had been crippled from birth, was magnificent on his guitar and sang with such a rich voice. Coming out of the South, Chicago and Detroit, he was a real true folk artist. He had chosen to hook himself up with Sonny Terry, who was blind and who had this wonderful voice and played a harmonica unlike anyone else in the world.

Sonny Terry and Brownie McGhee were two of the most worshiped folk artists of the period. When I went to Sonny Terry and Brownie McGhee and told them of the ambitious project that we were embarking on and the work that we wanted to do, they not only committed to doing it, but they found it an excellent opportunity to document and preserve the work within a context that they had not experienced before. Within the scope of this work, which is an arc of the music of Black people in America from East to West and North to South, their presence was a very critical voice.

Listening to the Basie Band, I once heard the great singer Joe Williams, who, to me, was the quintessential voice of Black expression—a resonant, deep baritone, almost bass sound, that had the capacity to interpret the music of his culture, his people. At the same time, it had a refinement that made you just delight in his enormous range and his musical and expressive ability. When I explained the idea of this project to Joe, he, like the others, said he would like to leave his footprints in that sand.

He came on board and sang two of the most beautiful songs on the album. We had the full benefit of hearing Joe Williams sing in ways that you would never hear in any of his other recordings. The soulful and plaintive quality that he brings to his expression of the material, and the richness of subtext, as well as the pain that is embodied in the songs that he sings were just glorious to hear. It is just wonderful to hear Brownie McGhee, with his folk guitar, and Joe Williams singing. You have this moment that's just incredible.

To me, then and now, one of the greatest voices that came out of Black culture was that of a young woman by the name of Gloria Lynne. Her range was so vast that I thought some of these songs, in her hands, going through her filter, would be a wonderful experience for the listener. She was very popular in American pop culture at that time. I went to Gloria and she listened to the material, and like Joe Williams and others, she said, "What is there here not to say yes to? Of course, I'll do it." She came to the songs with tremendous dignity and enormous integrity, and labored over every nuance of what she did—and did it magnificently.

Certainly no group, no collective did more to express the unfiltered, untampered art of Black expression on this album than did Bessie Jones and all of those who made up her community from the Georgia Sea Islands.

"YOU HEAR SONGS THAT WERE SUNG BY THE CHILDREN OF THE VILLAGES OF AFRICA, WHEN IT WAS A FREER AND HAPPIER TIME."

When the overture was first made to them to come, I remember that the idea of flying, alone, was enough to have a no-deal: They did not want to fly. They had never come out of the Georgia Sea Islands, and here they were coming to New York, to Webster Hall, to sing on this album, which, for many, was the first time ever recording. Getting Bessie Jones and the people of the Georgia Sea Islands was perhaps the biggest single victory of the work.

Through the history of slavery, which was replete with the misery of experiences that were daily unfolding in the lives of Black people, there was always the desire, the prayer, the hope and the wish for escape. In escaping from the plantations of America, many of the slaves left the mainland not knowing how to charter their way across the Atlantic to get back to Africa, as many wanted to do even after all these generations of distance from their place of origin. They wound up, instead, on this cluster of islands off the coast of the Carolinas and Georgia, called the Georgia Sea Islands.

Here, not only did many Black slaves run away and take up their lives, but eventually, in pursuit of the runaway slaves, whites began to populate the Georgia Sea Islands, which were ultimately turned into plantations themselves. The Blacks who lived on these islands were then conscripted into work.

The Georgia Sea Islands are very unique in that they remain, to this day, the repository of much of the original voice of slavery, the original voice of the post-slavery period, and the original voice of the music that accompanied people who populated this region. Within the Georgia Sea Islands, you find songs from Africa, some of it sung with many authentic nuances and in the original tongues. These come, for the most part, from the Gold Coast, or western coast of Africa, where much of slavery was derived. And many of the early religious songs of the slaves can be found on the Georgia Sea Islands, almost uncorrupted, untouched by other succeeding histories.

They all came up to New York—including the children. What a wonderful group of youngsters they were. And when they came, we spent endless days listening to the repertoire that Bessie Jones and these other artists had to offer, as well as the songs sung by the children, which were some of the earliest plantation songs of rural Black America. Much to our delight and our sense of reward, we captured all of it—all that we could possibly dream of.

I am privileged to have been given the opportunity to perform a couple of cuts on the album, which I delighted in—and in which I was instructed by Bessie Jones. It was also wonderful to feel the warmth of Joe Williams and to work with Brownie McGhee, Sonny Terry and all of the other artists. So many of them would do solo work throughout. There are many who never got to become very popular, but will always be remembered when people hear their work.

Once the arrangers and performers were in place, the musical selection process became the next priority. The first cuts are of the music of the cultures from which slaving was derived—the cultures of West Africa. You hear songs that were being sung by fishermen and warriors. You hear songs that were being sung by those who worked the land and tilled the soil. You hear songs that were sung by the children of the villages of Africa, when it was a freer and happier time.

The music in the first section of this anthology is sung in the original languages spoken by those who derived from the various cultures in Africa. And what you find, as you listen to the music chronologically, is that there are vocal nuances in the latter part of the musical journey—many generations removed—that are exactly the same as those originally sung by the peoples of Africa.

The French influence on Black slaves in Louisiana, before the Louisiana Purchase, brought another dimension to the United States. The Creole church music of early Louisiana is very different from the Black church music of the Georgia Sea Islands, Mississippi, Alabama and other Southern states. It is Catholic, which gives it a rather baroque French style. The music of the Roman Catholic order brought to the slave voice a whole other kind of musical sound, which is beautiful to hear in the cathedrals of Louisiana. But as we move into the early periods of the slave rebellions, we hear the songs of the slave beginning to take on another dimension.

In the music of the Civil War, you hear the richness of those who, with great pride, fought as Black units in

"THE EARLIEST ROOTS OF THE BLUES AND OF JAZZ, AS WE KNOW THEM TODAY, ARE THE EARLIEST ROOTS OF DEFIANT SECULAR MUSIC."

the segregated Union Army. You hear these men who, in their songs, reflected the pride of surviving slavery, and the pride of their mission, as ex-slaves, to bring America to a place that is permanently devoid of slavery. They hoped to find a new day of integration, where they could work themselves into the fabric of the nation and become part of the citizenry of this country. Songs like "We Look Like Men of War"—what a glorious song that was—reflected the pride that they felt. This song, which derived from religious text, was used by a group of warriors who were on their first mission in battle as part of the Union Army.

Then we move into the period right after the Civil War. There was great festive and joyous celebration in the churches because of the overthrow of slavery following Lincoln's Emancipation Proclamation. People sang to the new promise, the new day. The spirituals and other songs that came out of that time are replete with a great sense of not only the divine power, the divine intervention and the freeing of slaves, but also the mission for the future, the rejoicing in what we wanted to become as a people and as a nation. But with all of the expressions of hope to be found within that music, nothing had prepared the slaves for the harshness of what was to come right after.

America had not surrendered its racist beliefs and feelings. Although, now, it could no longer have an official relationship to slavery, it designed and ordered new laws that became laws of segregation, laws of containment, laws that severely limited opportunity, and very much reflected the slave state—with all of the aspirations of the slave state, but without the responsibility of having to care for the slaves.

Now, all of these men and women were just thrown into society at large. And society at large had no program, no respect, and no desire to absorb these citizens into their communities. So, Black people were left on their own, to their own devices.

Since it was particularly impossible to live within the law, because the laws were so oppressive and so brutal, many had to live outside the law. And the minute you were forced to live outside the law, you were punished by the rules of law, by the rules of justice. As a result, America developed a huge prison population, and from this new population came new voices, new thoughts, new rebellion, new longing and new loneliness. From this came the most unique of all Black musical forms: the songs of the chain gang.

The earliest roots of the blues and of jazz, as we know them today, are the earliest roots of defiant secular music. What came out of the prisons of America, out of the chain gangs, were some of the most glorious songs of Black experience, some of the most articulate expressions of rebellion against slave existence and prison existence. From this also came some of the greatest artists.

Even today, there are an inordinate number of prisons being built in this country, and the number of Black people who make up the prison population is greatly disproportionate to its population as a whole. When you think that there are more young Black men and women in the prisons of America today than there are in its universities, you begin to understand the relationship that Black people have always had to prisons and prison life, and it becomes clear how so much of our culture springs out of that world. The experience of a people who have been so harshly and cruelly treated for many centuries reflects back upon America's culture.

That such art could come out of that kind of oppression is in itself miraculous. But it does. When you hear Val Pringle sing the chain-gang songs and the work songs—with their rhythms and counter-rhythms, as well as the way in which the harmonies move in counterpoint—you are able to hear the true richness of that material.

Part of what the Black experience did for America was to create jazz, which many people identify as a truly original American art form—the music of the Black people, not a conglomerate of the music of Europeans. Through jazz, the new cultural voice of America was being expressed. Not that all of the music of Europe was lost—because certainly the music of Bach, Beethoven and Mozart is resplendent in its place in American expression across the board, regardless of race—but more specifically, within Black music itself, these European harmonies, these European overlays, and the music of the church began to find nuances within the more powerful expression of African culture. Thus, a rather unique phenomenon emerges called Black music, Black art, Black culture, Black spirituals, Black jazz. The blues is a strange amalgam of diverse music. And this music has lasted to this day.

Rap culture, which comes out of the prison culture, the culture of the inner cities, and of the ghettoes, is not unlike the traditional expression of the music of Black people. Rap is the young people's extension of the spoken word, the griot, the storyteller, who passes on the history of a people through the spoken tongue. There is nothing unique in what is being expressed here. It is almost a reaching back by a people to express a thing, to express views of the conditions in which they live, very much like their forefathers did.

Breakdance contains many of the same unique movements as were found in the African dance of the forefathers on the plantation. The vocal cadences of rap also reflect back to plantation songs.

"WE WILL CLIMB THIS LADDER TO A HARMONIOUS PLACE WITHIN THE AFFAIRS OF HUMANKIND."

When you listen to Bessie Jones on the earliest cuts of the album, when she does her preaching, begging God on the New Year's Day celebration to come and deliver us, one finds the same style there as is found within rap culture. It's a remarkable link. Yet the absence of a historical context to shed light on the meaning of all this music is what diminishes people's capacity to delight in it.

This anthology ends at the threshold of the 20th century because so much of the music from the dawning of the 20th century on has already been notated. Certainly, the rising up of the young orchestras of the period—the Jelly Roll Mortons, the Louis Armstrongs, Dixieland—all of that was recorded. We felt, therefore, that the appropriate time for closure of this work would be at the end of the 19th century. However, in that context, we were aware that so much of what was going on in the 20th century was still strongly reflective of and linked to what had gone on in the centuries that preceded ours.

This was not a weekend experience. We spent years at Webster Hall working on this project, getting the Bessie Joneses, finding the right individual voices, and doing all of this under technological circumstances that were far, far more primitive than anything we know today: There was one microphone sitting in the center of a room through which all voices and all things were heard. And yet, listen to the values captured by these technicians who had a tremendous genius for how to adjust and to move sound around in space. Webster Hall is a room with an acoustical environment whose only equal in all of America is Carnegie Hall.

This project was going on at a time when America was in the midst of yet another upheaval around the issue of race: the Civil Rights movement. Black citizens, after all these centuries, were still on this long road to freedom, and were still knocking at the door of the privileged to ask, how much longer must we be denied our human rights? How much longer must we be denied our civil rights? How much longer can you deny your moral responsibility to fellow beings? How long must we rebel? How long must we struggle to gain our dignity and our rightful place within the affairs of the family of humans?

While we were doing this work, Dr. Martin Luther King was preaching throughout the length and breadth of this nation. Martin and I were very close in our relationship to the Civil Rights movement, and on one occasion, I prevailed on Dr. King to give us permission to use one of his speeches as a song that would provide a link between not only the music of the anthology and the history of the day, but also as a link to what was going to be much of the future of America—because we still had not dealt with race in the most honorable sense. There are still issues of race and racism.

During one moment on the album, the choir sings to Black hopes and aspirations that the gates of heaven will open to us—that we will climb Jacob's ladder. We *will* climb this ladder to freedom. We will climb this

ladder to a harmonious place within the affairs of humankind. We call upon Dr. King, speaking in the last half of the 20th century, still asking for the fulfillment of claims that we have made upon our government, our nation, our fellow citizens, as our rights as a people.

You will hear the richness of the Black voice without violence, although we were caught up in so much violence—violence that we, too, brought to the table, in our rebel cause. But most of our evolution and our quest for freedom has been through a nonviolent mission. That is reflected in our music. We seek the truth of the better definitions of Christian philosophy. All men are brothers. All people are equal.

One should not be denied honor because of race or gender. What a simple concept this is, yet how difficult it is to attain. And for a work to try to reflect all of this while offering simple listening pleasure is in itself an awesome task. But if George Marek, who was very much my partner in seeing the fulfillment of this, were alive today, he would say it is an honorable thing that has come to closure. At last, this has come for the benefit of the listeners and for those who will read the text. You will find, in all of this, a moment in which to reflect on the history of a people. You will also find a great humanity and, I think, a great work of art. This is one of the most rewarding times of my life. I'm glad that I am here to see it take flight.

Spirit

"Can't do nothin' till the comes."

The Long Road to Freedom: An Anthology of Black Music is a re-creation of African-matrixed music in various performance settings by accomplished professional vocalists and instrumentalists; it is music that predated the era of sound recording. By 'African-matrixed,' we mean 'African-rooted,' 'Africa as origin,' 'evolved from an original African form,' and, as we enter the millennium and respond to the simple need to be better informed, to know more about many things, in this instance, the evolution of Black music, we understand we must begin at the source; there, we will find the cultural infrastructure of music, literature, visual art and dance that has its nexus on the African continent.

From the beginning, that infrastructure, in its various forms, whether tonal, written, physical or visual, spoke to and for the group, interpreting for them their remembered history, their past triumphs and pitfalls, their present mores and ways of being, as well as their goals and directions. That language, whether tonal, written, physical or visual, even if conceived by an individual, required endorsement by the group in order for it to become classic or traditional.

Of the various forms within the infrastructure, music, engaging the sensibilities in the all-consuming and powerful ways that it does, is clearly the most demanding, the most overtly convincing.

We can speak of origins, of pre-dynastic visual art and music, of a tradition of written African letters over 5,000 years old and, due to the group's endorsement of all that, we can, even in this millennium, touch and see and listen to the residuals of that cultural infrastructure and to the spinoffs that time has spawned. It is possible to argue that the evolution of that African-matrixed infrastructure occurred in three major phases: The first, a Phase of Celebration and Instruction; the second, a Phase

of Encounter with non-African social and political systems, and the third, a Phase of Affirmation and Realignment.

This collection, attempting as it does to present a comprehensive view of the evolution of African-matrixed music, must factor in, early on, the significance of dispersion and dislocation in the cultural life of a national group. Therefore, Phase Two, the encounter of Africans and persons of African descent with non-African sociopolitical and economic systems becomes critical to our examination of music that began as an African cultural form.

I argue that creativity is the reaction of the human spirit to the variety of its experiences, and that the reaction is expressed in many ways: in visual art or anarchy, in music or dance, in literature or love, or in violence. The removal of choice over one's life and of power over one's self would have been as catalytic to the captives then as it is to those of us who listen to the music now. Therefore, the reaction of the human spirit to the involuntary nature of forced dislocation and to the imposition of structured brutality and the dehumanization necessary to keep order and to quell

the rebelliousness, the constant resistance and the anarchy such a captive group would present suggests a need, ever-present in the slaveholders' minds, for an assault, unrelenting and focused, to bend the captives to the 'master's' will. The assault was structured and unparalleled, addressing, as it did, three areas of the enslaved Africans' milieu: their minds, bodies and, inevitably, of course, their environment.

> **"The removal of choice over one's life and of power over one's self would have been as catalytic to the captives then as it is to those of us who listen to the music now."**

Slaves, **submit** yourse

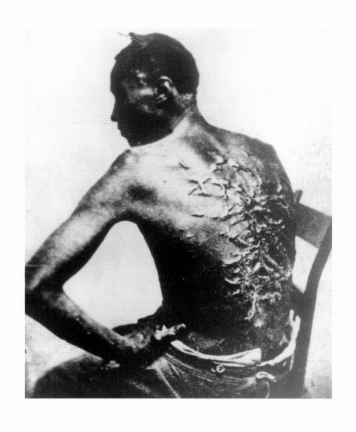

lves

to your masters, with all respect,

not only to those who are **considerate,**

but also to those who are **harsh.**

—Ephesians 6:5

A classic example of the assault on the minds of the captive Africans is "The Sermon" (in "Amazing Grace"), selectively interpreted from Ephesians 6:5 or 1st Peter 2:18.

The 'selling' of selected tenets of Western religion to a national group that had a belief system already in place, whose basic spiritual concepts are known to predate similar Western concepts, is analogous to the process discussed by Chancellor Williams in his seminal volume, *The Destruction of Black Civilization*. Williams called the process of control by substituting one form of thought for another "naming."

One is reminded of Police Chief Gillespie's shrewd forestalling of an outraged Virgil Tibb's precipitous departure from an understaffed police department in the movie *In the Heat of the Night*. As chief, Gillespie, played by Rod Steiger, subtly 'informs' the exiting detective of his 'real identity' by pointedly intoning, "All right, officer." The phrase would hang in the Southern air, and Tibbs, played by Sidney Poitier, his notion of self and responsibility effectively confronted and redirected, would reluctantly turn from the half-open door and

remain in the situation, mind and body in the service of the chief.

"Slaves, obey your masters in all things," was the actual exhortation that rang from one Southern gathering to another whenever slave masters allowed their captives to rest from their toil for a moment to receive, direct from the pulpit, focused indoctrination into the responsibilities of slavery: The concept 'This is God's will for you' was analogous to Williams' "naming," or substituting one form of thought for another.

The captives, however, created their own metaphors, and derived for themselves a healing paradigm: A God of redemption and salvation, a God whose love extended particularly to the downtrodden, a God of understanding and compassion. As they did so, they established a supportive liberation theology. A theology that began long before the Civil Rights Era with its promise of 'change on the way,' a God who would 'order (their) steps,' watch their backs and fill them with an energy that allowed them to proclaim, "Lord, I Don't Feel Noways Tired" (Disc 5) and to assure their fellow marchers and

the watching world, "I'll Never Turn Back No Mo'" (Disc 5), a theology that would sprinkle the long dusty road to Freedom with water from an empowering Deity.

Religious expression took on many forms. The spirituals branched out into several different musical modes, some lending themselves to elaborate arrangements, some were simply phrased narratives, others were pulsed by oppression, heavy with a recital of travail in bondage; and some were ecstatic affirmations of Freedom soon, of release and justice at the hands of a loving, all-seeing God. The notion of physical freedom from external control and spiritual salvation was generally held, and may be seen as the concept that enabled slaves to survive the long nightmare of brutally enforced servitude.

Captive Africans came to the Americas with a system of religiosity and spirituality well in place, a system that included belief in a Supreme Being, a Creation theory, and the concept of a sacred virgin birth. It was not hard to fit Western notions of Christianity into such a framework. The metaphors were interchangeable. However, the privilege of worship was not universal under slavery; some slaves were allowed, even encouraged, to worship, many others were savagely beaten if they were even suspected of clandestine worship. Thus, the advent of the 'invisible church.'

According to George Marek, president of RCA Records when this project was originally conceived, "The white man did not immediately recognize the totality of the African's religiousness, for even in Africa, before his introduction to (Western) Christianity, he attributed every detail of his existence to some level of godly intercession."

John Mbiti speaks of the many ways African people worshiped, of what he calls a corporate Faith, of their belief that "people are religious beings living in a religious universe…that there is a spirit world that differs radically from the human world (and) is invisible to the eyes of men…that man is forever a creature but he does not remain forever man."

Dr. Iva Carruthers sees slave religion, at least in part, as "theopraxis," that is, it contains certain characteristics that are indivisible with and inherent in slave life—a spiritual component, I would add, of the African-matrixed cultural infrastructure that enabled the slaves and their descendants not only to survive travail but to transcend, or to rise, Phoenix-like, from what were intended to be merely the ashes of their humanity.

One easily identifiable example of theopraxis is the ritual inclusion of traditional phrases, ideas or language in extemporaneous individual prayer. One such example is the "Prayer" (Disc 1) by a Georgia Sea Islands worshipper. Although original with the speaker, we find incorporated in the text, as was the custom, certain common and familiar phrases, as well as lines or ideas from favorite hymns or spirituals. Worshippers placed value on a speaker according to the reach and versatility of such inclusions and the depth of emotional waters into which the speaker could immerse the audience. The whole became, then, an example of what Stephen Henderson saw as Black linguistic virtuosity. To further identify the presence of structure in slave theopraxis, we look at the reprise, or replication, of traditional physical movements or patterns, as in the ring-shout; the ecstatic bent-knee forward leaps; and the up-tempo, feet together, backing movements that can be seen accompanying sermons or on the gospel stage.

In fact, the prayer, the spiritual and the shouts are the early believers' exuberant, anticipatory precursors of the mantra-like 'better-day-coming.' Faith, the enslaved worshippers concurred, was indeed 'the substance of things hoped for, the evidence of things unseen.'

Mbiti shares an African proverb that, however disseminated through the various ethnic or ontological ways of understanding humankind's relationship to God, provided, without a doubt, a psychological 'rock in a weary land': "The enemy prepares a grave, but God prepares a way of escape."

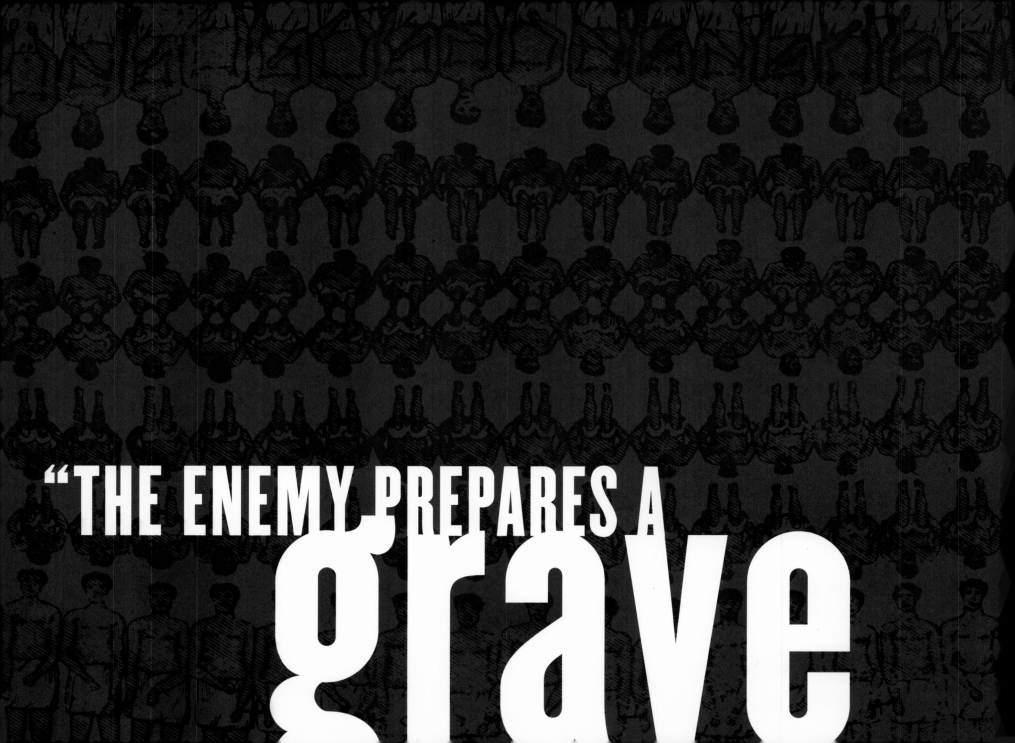

...but God prepares a way of escape."

Marek wonders how long it took to accept a Christian replacement of old forms, while some African American historians question the flow of religious thought, alleging it was originally from Africa to the West, rather than the reverse. Of interest is Dr. Yosef ben-Jochannan's comparative study of the works of Amenemope, Egyptian pharaoh, (*circa* 1300 BC) and King Solomon, (*circa* 970 BC). Interesting and provocative, it is a matter not likely to be resolved soon. At any rate, Marek argues that, in countries such as Brazil, Haiti and other arrival areas of the African diaspora, old African theological beliefs mix comfortably with Western Christianity.

In North America, Black leaders have been men and women of faith, from the Nat Turners and the Harriet Tubmans, to the Henry McNeil Turners and other historical figures and contemporary leaders. There have always been those of faith who led the community to 'the Rock' in its quest for shelter and for strength in its ongoing struggle to liberate itself.

That view, replicated almost two centuries later in the determined, almost ecstatic, voices of Dr. Martin Luther King's vast army of followers

Portrait of Huddie Ledbetter, "Leadbelly"

during the Civil Rights Era, along with today's more direct strategies, can be expected to continue in response to 21st-century oppressive forms.

It is impossible to explore the music in this collection and to fully experience its nuances without placing the men, women and children who created the music within a discussion of the music itself.

The work heard in this collection, from the Conversion section on Disc 1 through the music of the Civil Rights Era is music re-created by descendants of those early African captives, color-coded citizens still engaged in overcoming the angst of oppression while experiencing the paradox of some joy, some freedom, some prosperity, and

some enormous delight. It is a diasporic mix that challenges the listener's senses.

Harry Belafonte recalls his emotions: "I began to dig more deeply into Africa for the richness that came out of that culture, out of that continent....As I travelled into the world of the Georgia Sea Islands; as I delved deeply into the music of Leadbelly and the chain-gang experience of Black Americans; as I entered into the heart of the labor movement and went into the mines of Appalachia in West Virginia; and as I heard what the miners had to say—miners whose music came from Ireland, from Whales, even from Germany—the richness that came out of these cultures began to bathe me so fully, that I was very heady with the joy of it all." And what he delighted in was "America's willingness to hear the music of the culture of other people."

Belafonte credits both Paul Robeson and George Marek with being his mentors. Marek "helped guide me through any difficulties I might have encountered at RCA Records," as he pursued his dream: the collection you are about to enjoy.

"...African people carried on an internal dialogue about what it meant to be human, about morals and ethics, about ambition and triumph..."

Harry Belafonte recalls that, as a child of West Indian parentage growing up in the midst of Harlem, he was filled with wonder at the richness and the variety of cultures that swirled around him. "Not only was there a West Indian community… but I could hear Cubans all day long playing Latin music…folks from the English-speaking Caribbean playing the music of the lower Caribbean," and praise songs spilling their exuberance from African American churches. Figuring prominently in this heady cultural mix was the famed Apollo Theatre, itself a mecca for the "great orchestras and the great popular artists of the day, who brought the influences of jazz along with the nuances and

dimensions of popular culture from around America that were rooted in the Black experience." These were to be life impressions that were shaping, and that left Belafonte "quite fascinated by how little America knew about the culture of its Black citizens," and that we knew so little of ourselves. He vowed to change that. He embarked on a life of cultural enrichment, rife with exposure to artists such as Billie Holiday, Lester Young, Woodie Guthrie, Pete Seeger, Josh White and Leadbelly, a remarkable, wonderful man who had been released twice from prison, where he was serving life on the chain gang. Belafonte also came under the influence of Paul Robeson. Despite developing his skills and gifts and studying at the New School for Social Research, Belafonte still found it difficult to find work. He "fell into the world of music," became a popular performer, was sought out and signed by RCA Records, and in time had a critical, life-changing dinner with the then-president of RCA Records—writer, musicologist, and scholar, George Marek.

Marek was impressed with Belafonte's passionate desire to expose America and the world to the

drama and excitement of the music of the Black experience, and, convinced of the validity of that goal, he intervened and cleared the way for Belafonte's initial folk music LP, *Calypso*, which became the first album in the history of the business to sell a million copies in one year.

Speaking of the reasons he believed so staunchly in the value of the collection, Marek stated, "It is a listening experience of beauty, of sweetness, and of joy; even fun. Given its fidelity to the experience, anger, resentment and suffering are here as well. The listener can expect to find much unfamiliar and astonishing material, though some familiar favorites have been included."

The songs present a mélange of emotions and captivate the listener's spirit. It is through the dialogue he has with his culture—his spiritual beliefs, his arts, his athletics, and of course, through violence—that the oppressed relieves himself of the stress and tension imposed by the presence of the oppressors and the involuntary, unavoidable interaction with the dynamics of the oppressors' systems. So it was with the African captives-turned-slaves, and now with their descendants. This collection is compelling precisely because of the wide range of emotions one experiences, as new and exciting selections from that dialogue unfold.

If, from predynastic times and the early periods of African high civilization, African people carried on an internal dialogue about what it meant to be human, about morals and ethics, about ambition and triumph, about war and peace, about love and sadness, about anger and joy, about all these way stations along the path to spiritual attainment on which the ancients, given the magnificence of their accomplishments, seemed to be walking; if this dialogue was shared through their very effective cultural infrastructure of music, art, literature and dance, we can suppose that Phase One, which existed on the continent prior to any major impingement by non-African elements, laid a cultural foundation of unparalleled beauty and substance.

Eclectic and necessarily diasporic, given the dispersion of African people, the collection contains representative examples of African-matrixed music from a plethora of geographic locales. Each example

has been impacted and shaped by the sociopolitical rigors and limitations of that area. Even today, geography influences the quality of life. To be a slave in Boston was very different from being a slave in Mississippi, just as slavery in 18th-century New Orleans, with its access to Congo Square's music and slave vendors, its dances, musical instruments and songs, was quite different from the limitations imposed by 19th-century New Orleans, when an American approach to slavery prevailed, and Congo Square, as a place of retained African cultural expressions and small private slave enterprise, was no longer allowed. The Creole songs in this collection suggest that earlier, happier time.

Earliest known record of Black army musician, trumpeter Nero Benson, in Framingham, Massachusetts.

This collection has been ten years in the making. A staff under the direction of Harry Belafonte encountered many difficulties as they worked to identify material, to authenticate it and to find artists who could perform the music with the fidelity it deserved. It would be impossible to overstate the importance of one man, Leonard de Paur, to the overall creation and production of the collection. The legendary de Paur played a major role in researching, as well as arranging, directing and contributing enormously to the collection's written text.

More than ten artists make featured and solo appearances. They range from Harry Belafonte to Brownie McGhee to Sonny Terry; from Leon Bibb to Bessie Jones; from folk whose contributions are those of memories: blues and ballads handed down during their childhood, spirituals and work songs shared by parents and grandparents, to people whose names resonate through today's broad musical spectrum.

Universities and research centers opened their archives as researchers traveled to such diverse places as the Georgia Sea Islands, to Guinea on the west coast of Africa, to New Orleans, and even to a prison in Atlanta. Their determination to locate people who still knew the traditional forms paid off. They found men and women, many of them elderly, who remembered; who could recall songs handed down to them from the elders. Guardians of the culture, they could and did provide valuable linkage, generation-to-generation sharing, the way a people have always preserved tradition.

Researchers never lost their commitment to authenticity. At one point, a group of African musicians arrived in New York's harbor on a freighter from Ghana. Within a few hours, they were inside a studio recording the Ghanian music you can hear in The Roots (Disc 1).

This collection brings you some of the magic moments of music history. You will hear fine 20th-century artists performing chants, praise songs, hollers, ballads, war chants and hymns that were a traditional part of the ways our ancestors encouraged and empowered each other as they fought their way through the challenges of a chaotic society, sometimes losing touch, never losing hope, and seeming, somehow, to always summon the strength to find the joy and the music through the worst of it.

The collection illuminates many areas, not only the African plain and the Southern plantations, but also the Creole country, the children's playgrounds of New England, the Georgia of the Georgia reels, the small-town churches, the open roads where the nucleus of a great transportation system was being laid, where railroads were being built on the backs of chain gangs and Asian labor, the forests of West Virginia, and the city of Richmond, when Lincoln visited after Appomattox. Marek would emphasize that selections were made on the basis of whether the piece was musically interesting. Belafonte, while sharing that concern, was also passionate about authenticating the African roots of the material, about establishing a credible continuum that spoke to the many diasporic elements that comprise the Black sociopolitical and cultural experience. He wished to demonstrate, as powerfully and unequivocally as possible, evidence of African-matrixed music and its pervasive effect within the society.

1770

Crispus Attucks, who had earlier escaped from his slaveholder in Framingham, Massachusetts, is the first person killed in the Boston Massacre. The American Revolution begins.

"Popular music of our day, good and bad, could not exist without the antecedent of Black or African-matrixed music."

George Marek, of Austrian extraction, was impressed by the enormous influence African American music had on musicians who were not Black. He cites, among many, a young Stephen Foster; the son of the mayor of Allegheny, Pennsylvania; and "one Antonín Dvořák, who, in an article in the *New York Herald* in 1893, called attention to 'the beautiful Negro music of America.'"

Marek states that Dvořák's *Symphony From the New World* was in part, at least, the result of the inspiration he "received from what he heard here."

Marek goes on to assert that "calypso (and other West Indian music) was influenced by African American music, and, conversely, calypso then emigrated to the United States." A counter opinion would be that West Indian music itself was African-matrixed as a direct result of the original import of African captives to this continent and the compelling and dramatic impact of African musical sensibility on the indigenous Euro-musics of that region. There is no contradiction, however, to the enormous popularity of the Afro-Cuban, Afro-Latin or other Afro-inspired Latin musics as they immigrated to the United States and were enthusiastically welcomed into the African American community and embraced by other American music aficionados.

Marek speaks of the overwhelming influence of African American music's discrete musical nuances, and the Black experience itself, on Gershwin and his *Concerto in F*, his *Rhapsody in Blue*, and *Porgy and Bess*. He also refers to the development of jazz from earlier Black music as a completely original facet of American music. We concur with Marek that popular music of our day, good and bad, could not exist without the antecedent of Black or African-matrixed music. He goes on to say that "The Beatles, Simon and Garfunkel, Jefferson Airplane, Elvis and a legion of other non-Black musicians and composers "all must and many do acknowledge their debt to the sounds that were heard long ago on the plantations."

Eli Whitney patents the cotton gin, pushing cotton to the top of the list of cash crops and creating a voracious demand for slave labor.

THE ROOTS

The collection begins with tribal chants that date back at least to the 17th century. Those used here are known to have existed during the years when the sale and trade of free African people was viewed as merely a commercial process. The newly enslaved left behind a scenic homeland, beloved kin and treasured objects, carrying with them only their intellect, their strength, the infrastructure of their culture and their courage. This program contains aspects of their music that have been preserved. We hear an Ashanti war chant from Ghana, work songs from Nigeria and the Congo, "Homage to a King" from the Yoruba, harvest festival songs from Ghana and children's play songs from Ghana and Nigeria. There is an early hymn in a transitional language that is a mixture of African and English.

"The newly enslaved

left behind a scenic homeland,

beloved kin and treasured objects,

carrying with them only their intellect,

their **strength**,

the infrastructure of their culture and their courage."

CLOCKWISE FROM LEFT **D'Mba Mask**, Simo Society, Baga People, Guini, West Africa, 20th century, The Newark Museum; **Yoruba Beaded Container and Cover,** Christie's Images/Superstock; **Toy Fishing Boat**, Fante people, Ghana, West Africa 20th century, The Newark Museum; **King's Crown**, Yoruba people, Nigeria, West Africa, 20th century, The Newark Museum; **Yoruba Drum** for Ifa Ijebu area, Christie's Images/Superstock.

> # "...these poignant wakes bound the Black community with a sense of identity equaled by nothing else in their mutilated culture."

Although traditionally an Ashanti war chant, "Ose Yie," as with many songs of the people, can be used appropriately in any number of situations, serving always as a call for unity, whether in war, to enlist the group's support for a common concern; to announce the approach of a fearful animal or an enemy; to advocate a particular political posture or even to support one athletic team over another. Loosely, the question is, "Are you with us?"

The function of work songs varies little from one culture to another, and the same may be said of children's play songs; the Ga songs (Disc 1) are no exception. The emphasis in "Ashiee Tatale" is on a favorite delicacy: fried plantain.

"Oba Oba," on the other hand, serves as a praise song, announcing the approach of an honored guest or an important person. It also serves to keep alive the memory of a celebrated Yoruban leader.

In exploring the matrix of "Falle-well Shisha Maley," the transitional or mourning hymn that we hear, Winifred Vass speaks of the Bantu custom, related by the Abbe Proyart, of holding nightlong gatherings when death is imminent or recent; and, when a person is sick, "of summoning, with the physician, a band of musicians who assemble around his house and play on instruments incessantly day and night, presumably until the patient is recovered or dead." In slave life, this nocturnal practice of observing the

approach of death was preserved by members of the community of all ages, coming "to sing their most mournful hymns" as they sat on the floor inside the hut or stood around the hut, outside. Vass introduces an additional account of the observance as a Gullah practice: The drums of death would also sound, summoning to the 'settin-up' or wake. There would be hot drinks, and the drum would instruct the mourners as to when they should lie flat on their faces on the ground, when they should rise, when they should dance around the grave, and when they should sing.

Winifred Vass suggests that "Shisha Maley" is often mistakenly interpreted as "Sister Mary." It derives, instead, from the Bantu terms used for the traditional African form of mourning: *Kutshisha* (to be awake all night, to stay awake until the light of day), and *kakutshisha*. He argues that the line, "I love Shisha Maley, yes I do," does not refer to a particular person, "but to the whole heartwarming gathering of bereaved friends," and that "these poignant wakes bound the Black community with a sense of identity equaled by nothing else in their mutilated [*sic*] culture."

The final song, "Amazing Grace," was composed by the former slave trader John Newton, who left school at age eleven, became a corrupt seaman, and eventually, captain of a slave ship. He engaged in the trade and ferrying of African people under the most vile conditions. Finally, terrified by a storm, guilt-ridden and contrite, he converted to Christianity, studied for the ministry, and became a powerful preacher. To augment his ministry, he composed hymns, one of which was "Amazing Grace." It became a classic. Ironically, it brought much comfort to an enslaved people and retains that mantle of comfort today.

An unexpectedly rasping rendition of "Amazing Grace" is followed by a particularly devious sermonic text, a cynical coupling that shocks until the listener realizes that he or she has just undergone a slave experience—has felt personally assaulted, abraded, intellectually brutalized—thus forced, if only for a moment, to wear a suit of Negro cloth.

For more on the last selection, the infamous "Sermon," see the introductory narrative to this collection.

NEXT PAGE: detail from **Akunitam or "Cloth of the Great,"** Akan people, Ghana, West Africa, 20th century, The Newark Museum

Funeral in Virginia

SHOUTS & EARLY SPIRITUALS

S houts were the slaves' earliest linking of the newly imposed 'Christianity' with their African past, possibly the precursors of spirituals. Everything about them except the words suggests Africa. Used in 'praise houses,' they accompany the traditional African ring-shout, and, in the absence of the forbidden drum, they utilise "basers" to provide hand

and foot rhythm. Shouts even bear a name reflective of an African term that describes the same ring-shout pattern: "Saut," in which instance the African *s* is sounded [sh].

The practice of welcoming in the new year is common throughout the world, but as an African residual, the observance began hours before midnight with songs of praise and thanksgiving for having survived the past year, with shouts, prayers, and testimony regarding obstacles overcome. Finally, a watcher, posted for the purpose, would see the first faint rays of sunlight. The watcher's shout, in this instance the transcendent "Hark 'E Angel," is sung by Harry Belafonte. This announced, the gathering continued, often erupting into the jubilant "Yonder Comes Day," rife with the possibility that this New Year's Day might indeed herald better times ahead, and always, with shouts and prayers for God's continuing intercession and support, they would "sing in" the new year.

The meeting ended with the participants exhausted but filled with goodwill, with handshaking all around, and the final "Goodbye Ev'rybody," again,

a song with multiple interpretations. Sometimes in later years, a song that called down blessings on the gathering, such as "God Be With You 'Til We Meet Again," became an optional farewell. The tradition survived slavery.

In contemporary African American society, the 'ritualing' of watch meeting, or watch night, still occurs in Black churches across the country, whether elite or of the people. The meetings are announced from the pulpit or in the church bulletin, and the faithful are expected to attend. The mode of service remains very much the same as before.

Harriet Tubman, or "Moses," as she later became known, unable to persuade her brothers to accompany her, and afraid of betrayal if her escape plans were known by others, is said to have walked through town on the evening prior to her escape singing a similar song, "Goodbye, I'm Going to Leave You," even blatantly bowing low before her master as she passed him on her final trek down the road.

"Goodbye Ev'rybody" may be seen, therefore, as a 'mascon' song, that is, one that has a common theme with a multiplicity of applications.

Harriet Tubman

"Goodbye" was in all probability the saddest word in the slave's lexicon."

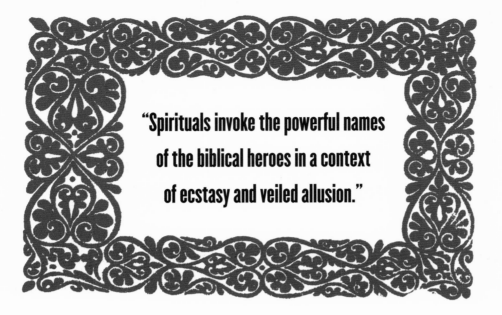

"Spirituals invoke the powerful names of the biblical heroes in a context of ecstasy and veiled allusion."

72

"shout," that is, dance his praise in a prescribed fashion leading to trance. The older shouts were dramatic; the dancers flapped their arms to imitate angels' wings or held out their hands as if reading from the Bible, like John the Revelator. The whole performance was extremely African in style. The participants danced in a loose circle, counterclockwise, in tight rhythmic coordination, but not in unison, each one improvising, in his own way, on the movement's pattern. They leaned forward facing the earth, knees bent ("gimme the kneebone bend"), feet flat to the floor, moving in a sliding, shuffling step, seldom lifting and never crossing their feet. Foot crossing, the prominent trait of European dance, was regarded as sinful and was forbidden in the "shout" or sacred dance of the Blacks.

"All dancers clapped and sang, their voices breaking out in individualized but familiar patterns of rhythm, melody, and changing vocal quality that complemented the lead. The short-phrased leader-chorus form, so typical of Africa, invited total participation and permitted endless experiments in syncopation, in brief tonal and rhythmic comment,

Suffice to say that "goodbye" was in all probability the saddest word in the slave's lexicon.

"Kneebone Bend," possibly one of the most fascinating of all spirituals, touches on so many elements of African/slave life that it becomes both mascon word and trope. The late Stephen Henderson, former Chair of the Humanities Department at Howard University, borrowed from NASA the word *mascon*, and in a brilliant stoke of Black creativity, applied the acronym to African American poetry and literature "to mean a massive concentration of Black experiential energy" that affects understanding of cultural elements within the African diasporic

infrastructure. Henderson, in speaking of mascon words, adds that they "cut across areas of experience usually thought of as separate....In fact, the meanings overlap and wash into each other on some undifferentiated level of common experience." "Knee" and "bone" appear repeatedly in the everyday as well as the ceremonial life of the African and the slave.

Alan Lomax, preeminent cultural anthropologist, writing of African and slave musics and ceremonies, says slave "spirituals invoke the powerful names of the biblical heroes in a context of ecstasy and veiled allusion. The earliest type (e.g. "Kneebone," "Daniel," and "Read 'Em, John") demands that the worshipper

in textual improvisation. During the service, the performance ran long—ten minutes to an hour—so that the brief melodies and their shifting polyrhythmic and polyparted support received a high polish before people sang and danced themselves out or got happy and shouted all over the church. Just as the singers were not restricted to one tonal quality but could play over the whole range of vocal qualities (moaning, cooing, sobbing, growling, and so on), so the dancers were not limited to repetitive movement but could break out into brief, surprising improvisations. Yet the whole group was united in its strict adherence to the beat of the feet on the floor and the orchestra of hands.

"This special amalgam of (early) Christianity and African religious style gave the blacks a feeling of unity, of hope, at times even of joy, in spite of slavery and its aftermath during Reconstruction. It also produced a large body of noble and touching songs, probably unmatched for singability and worldwide popularity. They came from people generally regarded in that period as ignorant, uncouth and hopelessly miserable. A good many were created on St. Simons

African Americans at prayer meeting, 1862

Island by the ancestors of (today's) singers and are still sung there beneath the moss-hung live oaks."

Alan Lomax goes on to describe the singing of "Kneebone," particularly as delivered by Joe Armstrong—the oldest, and, to Lomax, in many ways the best—who at ninety still had a voice of remarkable clarity and strength. "He had a strange and honeyed way of releasing a pitch, lowering it slightly and softening it as the other singers chimed in under him, one part after another, while the clapping hands wove together layers of crossed rhythms."

Lydia Parrish of St. Simons Island, wife of the painter Maxfield Parrish, learned of "another version of 'Kneebone' used for rowing, where the oarsmen bent to their knees. When this song was performed as a shouting spiritual, the singers bent their knees to lower themselves toward the ground, a piece of

choreography that is characteristically African. In fact, this seems to be (an early) piece, invoking the names of the ancestors, calling them morning and evening, then ceremonially requiring the worshippers to bend their knees to the earth in the traditional African gesture."

Creighton Churchill explains that, "when 'Kneebone Bend' was used for rowing, it could have had only one rhythmic accompaniment—the oars—since the other two rhythms, the hands and heels, would have thrown the rowers off their beat. The speed of the rowing version must also have been slower, for one could not possibly row to the rhythm of this version. It should be recognized, as well, that no musical meter known to man can represent exactly the rhythms of oars and their locks; in this song especially, it is something intangible and personal."

Jacqui Malone, in her brilliant work, *Steppin On the Blues*, explores the relationship of dance to music and to sculpture, and makes the point that "dancers (become) a magnificent form of sculptural art. Through dance, sculpture is recreated for public view. Africans brought to North America were no doubt affirming their ancestral values when they sang a slave song that urged dancers to 'gimme de kneebone bent.' To many western and central Africans, flexed joints represented life and energy, while straightened hips, elbows, and knees epitomized rigidity and death." Peter Wood argues that "the bent kneebone symbolized the ability to 'get down.'"

To further explore the notion of "bones" as a trope in the cultural infrastructure of the African diaspora, one recalls the classic sermon "Dry Bones in the Valley," and the equally classic spiritual, a traditional song that connects all of the body's bones and challenges the singer's memory. Contemporary historians and writers often speak, in requiem, of the whitened bones of our African ancestors that carpet the Atlantic floor from Goree to the Americas as a result of the Middle Passage, and of the bleached bones of those Africans who jumped overboard or were thrown to their deaths. Gamblers use the term 'bones' when throwing dice. Bones are a common and desirable artifact used by those involved in voodun. African craftspersons carve exquisite pieces of art from bones, often producing work that so closely resembles ivory, it is almost difficult to differentiate, and bones can be crafted for use as simple musical instruments. There are probably numerous other references that would apply.

Kneebone in the mornin'
Ah-ah, kneebone,
Bend my kneebone to the ground,
O Lord, kneebone bend.

Kneebone, didn't I tell you,
Ah, kneebone,
Kneebone, didn't I tell you,
O Lord, kneebone bend.

Kneebone, didn't I call you,
Ah-ah, kneebone,
Kneebone, didn't I call you,
O Lord, kneebone bend.

Kneebone, Zacharis,
Oh, kneebone,
Kneebone,
O Lord, kneebone bend.

The Supreme Court, in the Dred Scott decision, denies American citizenship to Blacks. Together with the passing of the Fugitive Slave laws and the Kansas-Nebraska Act, which opened up northern territory to slave owners, it ensured the survival of the "peculiar institution."

LOUISIANA CREOLE & SLAVE CHRISTMAS

When Alan Lomax discusses "Kneebone Bend," he leads us first through a truncated explication of African religion, saying that it involves "the active worship of high gods as creators of the universe, and of a pantheon of lesser immortals and ancestral spirits who control such elemental forces as fire, and water, and sex, and are ever-present participants in the affairs of their worshippers and descendants." He elaborates on this, touching on the effect that acculturation and the introduction of new languages had on styles of worship and music, particularly mentioning the Caribbean and the Creole.

Marek also speaks of the slaves held in French territory, particularly Louisiana, using French patois and, within that form, creating spirituals, love songs and other musical expressions. The Creole songs in the Louisiana Creole section represent that all-but-lost tradition of merging African residuals with language, music and the traditions of their French and Spanish owners.

Marek speaks of "Place Congo," the area in New Orleans set aside for the use of "slaves and free Black folk of every hue," who would come to congregate for a time of dancing, singing and general exuberance. Musical devices, usually forbidden, were allowed in Congo Square.

George Washington Cable, in a *Century Magazine* article dated February 1886, writes vividly of Congo Square. As a Southerner born in New Orleans and a Confederate Army veteran, his work has more than some validity. Bruce Jackson, the editor who included Cable's article in a contemporary anthology, agrees that "folklore (and music) found among Creole Negroes was very different from the Negro folklore (and music) found elsewhere in the United States. The fusion was with the French rather than the Anglo-Irish tradition." But, Jackson says, "The Creole tradition is an important one; in many aspects, it still survives, and we would lose an important point of reference if we did not have Cable's work."

At one point in his article, Cable says: "Up at the other end of Orleans Street, hid only by the old padre's garden and the cathedral, glistens the ancient Place d'Armes. In the early days it stood for all that was best; the place for political rallying, the retail quarter of all fine goods and wares, and at sunset and by moonlight the promenade of good society and the haunt of true lovers; not only in the military, but also in the most unwarlike sense, the place of arms, and of hearts and hands and of words tender as well as words noble.

"The Place Congo, at the opposite end of the street, was at the opposite end of everything. One was on the highest ground; the other on the lowest. The one was the rendezvous of the rich man, the master, the military officer; of all that went to make up the ruling class; the other of the butcher and the baker, the raftsman, the sailor, the quadroon, the painted girl, and the negro slave. No meaner name could be given the spot. The negro was the most despised of human creatures and the Congo was the plebeian among negroes.

OVER LEAF:
After the Sale,
market scene in Richmond, VA

NEXT PAGE:
The Bamboula,
Century Magazine

> "To consider, with any degree of integrity, what Christmas Day as occasion meant in the life of a slave is to enter a force field of incredible intellectual and emotional tension."

John Brown attacks Harper's Ferry in an antislavery revolt. Two and a half months later, Brown is hanged in Charleston, Virginia.

"The white man's plaza had the army and navy on its right and left, the courthouse, the council hall and the church at its back, and the world before it. The black man's was outside the rear gate, the poisonous wilderness on three sides…

"The booming of African drums and blast of huge wooden horns called to the gathering. It was these notes of invitation, reaching beyond those of other outlandish instruments, that caught the Ethiopian ear, put alacrity into the dark foot, and brought their owners, male and female, trooping from all quarters."

Cable, who became an émigré from Louisiana to Massachusetts because of his writings, goes on to describe the varieties of instruments, how they were used, and at one point, obviously in awe and admiration, says: "The result was called music." He gives an elaborate physical account of the slaves, of the dancing to the traditional "Bamboula," and finally shares with us a loose translation of "Miche Banjo," which provides a glimpse of the ongoing color/caste dialogue between Blacks of different hues; an ongoing residual of slavery instituted by the licentious use of power by white males; a power that rode roughshod across Black marital ties and through Black homes claiming possession, by divine right, over Black women of every age, even to the point of incest. The psychological damage was heightened by notions of superiority, privilege and the reality of blame that ricocheted between all parties involved, including many emotionally abandoned white women. "To be or not to be?"; a rhetorical question still only partially resolved at present.

> Look at that darky there, Mr. Banjo,
> Doesn't he put on airs!
> Hat cocked on one side, Mr. Banjo,
> Walking-stick in hand, Mr. Banjo,
> Boots that go "crank, crank," Mr. Banjo.
> Look at that darky there, Mr. Banjo,
> Doesn't he put on airs!

"Pour la belle Layotte," another of the Creole songs, describes the singer's ongoing search, "all around the town, for a girl to compare with his fair Layotte." "Yea," he sings, again and again, "for the fair Layotte I must crazy die. Yes, crazy I must die!"

The music in the Louisiana Creole section replicates the gaiety of Creole frolics, and the listener is party to the fun.

Cable, in his text, clearly sees no reason for animus in the color/caste dialogue, feeling that the participants are, genetically, half brothers. The issue brings to mind the moment when, in the heat of a post-Civil War Congressional debate, an irate pro-Black white legislator of some stature rose with the challenge that, in his opinion, there was no one there who could claim, with impunity, that their blood was free of any Negro taint [sic]. The record does not say that anyone responded to the challenge.

The Confederate Army attacks Fort Sumter.

SLAVE CHRISTMAS

To further explore the climate that fostered the music created by slaves, we can examine the validity of our notions regarding the ways slaves celebrated Christmas. Obviously, there was no single approach, and, unfortunately, many slave owners were violently opposed to exposing slaves to any aspect of religion; the narratives of the period are swollen with accounts of slaves flogged, even beaten to death for being caught praying or for stubbornly professing faith in God after being confronted with the offense. It is from this reality that we have learned of the 'invisible church,' and that we have found that slaves did indeed attempt to control and conceal the sounds of their praises or their implorations.

Therefore, to consider, with any degree of integrity, what Christmas Day as occasion meant in the life of a slave is to enter a force field of incredible intellectual and emotional tension. One is torn between a traditional perception of a day of hiatus in the midst of what has unequivocally been a year of trauma, particularly since one's deep desire is for some respite for the slave, a hope that each would have experienced some level of human beneficence. On the other hand there are the documents, the testaments that contradict that notion; there are firsthand accounts. When we resolve the yin and yang of this, we find a simple truth made of both: Slaves experienced Christmas according to what physical location they were in and under whose ownership, the latter being the most influencing element.

It was quite possible that Christmas could begin with an ambiance that had religious overtones; that demonstrated the owner's benevolence in acceptable ways, and that turned into a day of great festivity, with singing, dancing, fun and an overflow of food for all. Despite the fact that most slaves seemed to be heartfelt Christians, seemed to need a religious

base and to possess the intense levels of spirituality that mere survival demanded, firsthand accounts do not entirely support such a theory.

Howard Thurman refers to the spirituals as "watering places which affirm the spirit," as an oppressed people struggle to keep the faith while they fight against despair and the vicissitudes of American history." He argues that the genius of these religious folk songs stems from the individual's sense of being a child of God, and he makes the further argument that, in addition to what the slaves understood of the Old and New Testaments and the world of nature, the spirituals were driven by the common lot or inner life of the singers.

Christmas Day, it seems, was largely one of secular celebration and revelry. In fact, inebriation was not only allowed, but was an expected, even encouraged, part of the festivities. Many slave owners looked with suspicion on those slaves who refused the liquor and refrained from joining the revelry.

Frederick Douglas tells that it "was deemed a disgrace not to get drunk at Christmas," and was seen as rejecting the favor of the master. He tells of the various plans slaveholders used to encourage mass dissipation in order to disgust the slave with an overdose of what appeared to be 'freedom,' such as holding contests to determine who could drink the most without getting drunk. "So when the holidays ended, we staggered up from the filth of our wallowing, took a long breath, and marched to the field—feeling, upon the whole, rather glad to go…"

The secular approach to Christmas and the selective manner in which the Bible was taught to the captives may, Howard Thurman contends, account for the dearth of Christmas spirituals. The birth of Christ was certainly not taught as the advent of a Savior. The slaves, however, who had professed Christianity understood the event as sacred, as meaningful, and undoubtedly identified with the plight of the newborn's family, and welcomed the Birth in such songs as "Mary, What You Call Yo' Baby?"

Put in perspective, Christmas clearly was a day that came burdened with expectations from many sources. Prioritized, the day would yield first to the wishes and desires of the slave owner and his family, who might expect to entertain lavishly and provide,

according to custom, "gracious hospitality for relatives and travelers alike. "On a large plantation, a crowd of fifteen at breakfast was not uncommon, according to Catherine Clinton, author of *The Plantation Mistress*. Obviously, "traditional" Southern hospitality required the careful attention to detail, preparation and service that the system of slavery provided. Slaves pressed into such duty served long, stress-filled hours and had little if any time to join those of the community who, more fortunately, could enjoy, if permitted, the African-matrixed John Kunnering (or John Canoe)

festivities. Kunnering, according to all reports, consisted of slaves loosely parading behind a gaily-costumed 'negro King,' his colorful tatters flying, his followers 'playfully' threatening not to disperse until the white spectators joined the impromptu theatre by dispensing small gifts and favors to the crowd.

In a continuing effort to explore the wellspring from which slave music comes, we examine another aspect of slave life: As part of the annals of the Black slave experience, there is always the very real syndrome, as opposed to any notion of individual

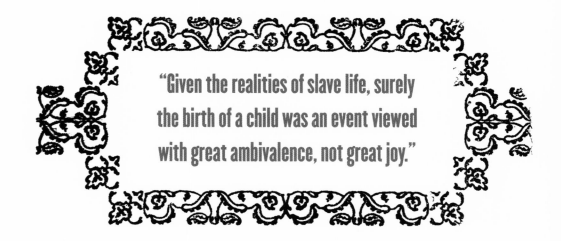

"Given the realities of slave life, surely the birth of a child was an event viewed with great ambivalence, not great joy."

caprice, of slave mothers asphyxiating or otherwise destroying an infant at birth in order to place it outside the systemic degradation of slavery, committing what may be seen by some, with certain justification, as an act of great moral courage, that is, sacrificing the child in order to save it from certain future outrage and debasement.

Therefore, given the realities of slave life, surely the birth of a child was an event viewed with great ambivalence, not great joy. In a society where childbirth was usually planned, but not by two willing participants; where conception was profit driven and where neither the hapless mother nor the father, as mere inseminator, had any control over the unlucky infant's destiny, it defies all logic to suppose that there was much joy over the birth of a child already destined for the market, the field or the big house, and certainly for early, usually ruthless, separation from its mother.

Available narratives contain very little about how slave men, forced to procreate for their master's profit, felt about the birth and fortunes of such children. Nevertheless children were objects of love and care by both men and women within the body of the slave community. Everybody was uncle or aunt because mother may have been sold away yesterday or beaten to death today. Frederick Douglas speaks of his separation from his mother while still an infant: "I never saw my mother to know her as such more than four or five times in my life." She lived about 12 miles from the infant Frederick, and "she made her journeys to see me in the night, on foot, after performing her day's work." He recalled hearing of her death after the event, and being relatively unmoved.

The records are heavy with accounts of slave infants sold for a dollar. Youngsters as young as six or seven were flogged, sometimes to death. Given the widespread exploitation and sexual abuse of children in today's society of laws (where accountability is still required, even if pro forma), it is impossible to contemplate the victimization of slave children of all ages and gender when there were no laws, only license—when the twisted inclinations of plantation owners, unrestricted, drunk with possibility, and flexing their omnipotence, became the shadowy social norm, a norm obviously under-documented because of its surreptitious viciousness.

If contemporary literature on abuse is any measure, the physical and psychological damage was enormous. Could this only partially hidden component of the inner-life of the slave be responsible for such classics as "Nobody Knows de Trouble I've Seen"? Where does one locate the adult slave in the creation of the song "Mary, What You Call Yo' Baby?" under such circumstances, except in the bone, the marrow of his/her humanity? Given the fact that the birth of Jesus was not taught as the advent of a Savior, from what incredible fountain does the ability to continue to express love and empathy, despite enormous personal abuse and loss, spring?

Lincoln signs the Emancipation Proclamation, freeing slaves in rebel states.

UNDERGROUND RAILROAD

& THE WAR

M usic was used to communicate; it did much more than pleasure the soul: it worked as a language. It was important to the success of the volunteer and dangerous system of the Underground Railroad.

These are some of the songs used to provide escaping slaves with information, to pass along warnings, escape signals and the like, or to cover up clandestine, escape-connected activities.

"Slaves worshipped wherever and as often as they could secretly gather."

Two classic spirituals appear here: "Steal Away to Jesus" and "Many Thousan' Gone." The latter, one of the saddest, most hauntingly beautiful expressions in the canon, speaks to loneliness imposed by the absence of those beloved, whether through torture or death, by sale or escape; it speaks to what is irreplaceable.

The spiritual "Steal Away to Jesus," as might be imagined, had ongoing import to the slaves. Not allowed to converse in the fields, they used songs to share information. Songs or segments were hummed or sung from one to another until the group understood that a meeting would occur in the plantation's 'invisible church' that night. The 'invisible church' was a fact of slave life, not a figment of some writer's imagination. Slaves worshipped wherever and as often as they could secretly gather. "Steal Away to Jesus," while unequivocally spiritual in intent, supported the slave's focus on death as surcease from travail, God as deliverer, and heaven as home. In another context, it was also a covert signal used to suggest the timeliness and wisdom of escape. Another interpretation might be escape motivated by an overwhelming fear of death at the hand of the slave owner or his minions.

2. *Green trees are bending,*
   Poor sinner stands a-trembling;
   The trumpet sounds within-a my soul,
   I ain't got long to stay here. Chorus

3. *Tombstones are bursting,*
   Poor sinner stands a-trembling;
   The trumpet sounds within-a my soul,
   I ain't got long to stay here. Chorus

4. *My Lord calls me,*
   He calls me by the lightning;
   The trumpet sounds within-a my soul,
   I ain't got long to stay here. Chorus

"Follow the Drinking Gourd," or Big Dipper, with its handle pointing North, is a careful directive full of cautionary advice for overcoming the perils of travel through unfamiliar territory without maps, friends, or any notion of the terrain and its dangers.

"There's a Meeting Here Tonight" was apparently useful in a number of ways as well. In all probability, it began as covert instruction sung as slaves labored in the fields, its strains faintly heard from a distance by those in the community, whose assignment was the 'big house.' Its religious significance to the slave, however, can in no way be diminished, nor can its enthusiastic adoption later, by the burgeoning labor movement's recruitment efforts, be overlooked.

2. *The riverbank will make a very good road,*
   The dead trees show you the way,
   Left foot, peg foot, traveling on,
   Follow the drinking gourd. Chorus

3. *The river ends between two hills,*
   Follow the drinking gourd,
   There's another river on the other side,
   Follow the drinking gourd. Chorus

4. *Where the great big river meets the little river,*
   Follow the drinking gourd,
   The old man is a-waitin' for to carry you
   *   to freedom,*
   If you follow the drinking gourd. Chorus

THE WAR

For nearly three years, the desire of Black men to participate in a war in which their freedom was only one of the major issues, was at fever pitch. They did what they could as "contraband," forging for food, horses and other supplies critical to the maintenance of an effective fighting force; in that invaluable role, the Union troops could not have succeeded without them. Finally, token enlistments were allowed, in time, troops were committed to battle, and Black men, under circumstances that were rarely equal, were able to continue a tradition of Black valor in war that began with those who followed Washington to Valley Forge, a tradition of bravery that continues to this day.

Pulsed by an incredible patriotism, the war songs, beginning with "The Colored Volunteer," are exciting beyond belief. Suppressed Black men, freedom in their eyes, declaring "We'll stand by the Union if we only have the chance," and daring to claim "The Union will be saved by the colored volunteer," is high musical drama.

The listener is indescribably moved on first hearing the barely distinguishable solo voice that raises the declarative "We look like men," the musical interval that introduces the powerful and poignant marching song of history's famed Black 54th Massachusetts Volunteer Regiment. Initially, it contains a very sensitive moment, but as the song gains momentum and cadence, it becomes increasingly overwhelming, and we are swept into the massed emotion of a legendary group of Black soldiers who not only declared themselves men, but defended that manhood by refusing the contemptuous partial pay that Congress allocated them as "laborers," not as soldiers. Subsequently, the men declined an offer of deficit pay negotiated by the governor and approved by the legislature of the state of Massachusetts.

Congress finally succumbed to pressure, and after 18 months of unsalaried soldiering, the men of the Fifty-fourth received the justice they sought. "We look like men," a power-filled statement of resolve is a worthy testament to the valorous men who sang it.

The regimental history of the legendary Fifty-fourth Massachusetts is itself stirring and moving. The first Black regiment to be formed in the North, the Fifty-fourth was the result of Massachusetts military

governor John A. Andrew's passionate response to the war effort, and his request to Secretary of War Edwin M. Stanton to be allowed to organize a regiment of colored volunteers who would serve for three years. Once granted permission, Andrew appointed George L. Stearns to head a committee of prominent citizens to superintend the project. The project, after six weeks of focusing primarily on Massachusetts, which had only a small Black population, had attracted less than one hundred volunteers.

Congress passes the Thirteenth Amendment, which, after ratification, abolishes slavery.

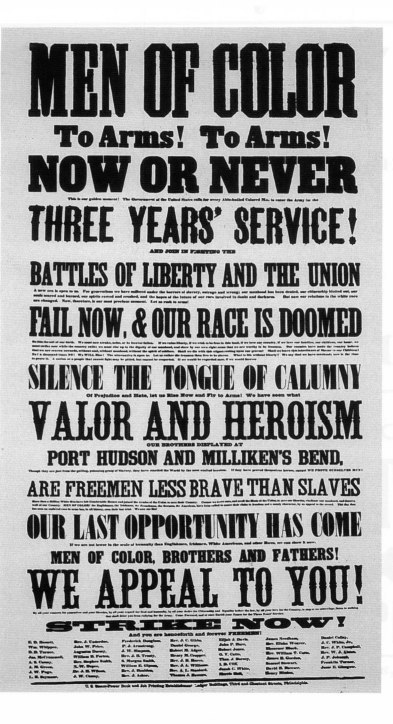

An appeal was made to Black leaders such as Frederick Douglas, William Wells Brown, Henry Highland Garnet, Martin R. Delany, J. Mercer Lansgton, Charles Lenox Remond, Stephen Myers, J. W. Loguen, and George T. Downing to act as recruiting agents. Newspaper ads were employed, and when these men of skill and substance added their eloquence and presence to the effort, enlistments soared. According to Benjamin Quarles, "The recruiters were required to write to Stearns every evening, giving a summary of the day's work, and to send in a statement of expenses every week.… In two months, Stearns had organized a line of recruiting posts from Boston to St. Louis (and) 1,000 Negroes representing every state in the country, plus a quota from Canada were learning the manual of arms at the camp at Readville, Massachusetts."

The commissioned officers, despite Black criticism, were white, young, and of an average age of twenty-three. Andrew's response to the criticism, Quarles tells us, was that he wanted only the highest type of men, since the Fifty-fourth was the first colored regiment to be raised in the free states and

> ## "We'll stand by the Union if we only have the chance."

would be, in essence, a very public experiment. Andrew wrote, according to Quarles, that he had in mind "young men of military experience, of firm anti-slavery principles, ambitious, superior to the vulgar contempt of colour, and having faith in the capacities of coloured men for military service." According to Quarles, Andrew approached Robert Gould Shaw as the likely candidate to command the newly formed Black regiment. Handsome, wealthy, "of great personal charm, and from a socially prominent family, he had attended school in Switzerland, college at Harvard," and by way of experience was, at the time, captain of the Massachusetts Second Infantry. After hesitating for a day, but being "naturally inclined toward difficult resolves," Shaw accepted, and in his wake there followed a number of other young men from well-to-do families. Shaw made major on April 11, colonel on May 13th, and, five days later, Secretary of War Stanton telegraphed Governor Andrew to notify the Fifty-fourth to report to Commander Hunter, Department of the South, at Hilton Head, South Carolina.

Benjamin Quarles gives us a definitive account of what occurred next, from which we excerpt the following:

"On that morning, Andrew, accompanied by nearly 3,000 visitors, including such notables as abolitionists William Lloyd Garrison, Wendell Phillips, and Frederick Douglas, went to the Readville Camp to present to the regiment four flags which friends had procured, among them was a national flag presented by the young colored women of Boston; another showing the state colors was a gift of the Colored Ladies' Relief Society, and a third, donated by a 'large and patriotic committee,' was an emblematic banner of white silk; and just as sure to catch the eye were the regimental banners of superb white silk, adorned on one side by the coat of arms of Massachusetts and on the other side by a golden cross and a golden star…to conquer by the sign of the cross was expressive of the belief that the mission of the Fifty-fourth was a holy crusade.

"The presentation ceremonies were impressive; ten days later, the Fifty-fourth received their orders and came to Boston to debark. Although scheduled to march directly to the wharf, so great was the public desire to see the Negro soldiers that a review had been arranged. On the morning of May 28, the city

had an expectant air. The national colors flew everywhere, as if in celebration of a holiday. One hundred policemen were on duty to clear the streets and keep order. Although not known to the public, additional reserves of police were held in readiness, for it was not certain how Boston, liberty-loving though it was, would respond to the novel sight of a thousand Negroes in military dress.

"The excitement mounted as the Negroes marched through the downtown streets on their way to the Common." And with today's understanding, we, privileged to hear their music on this rare collection, know how they styled.

"Thousands cheered the impressive spectacle (no such reception had been given to the preceding fifty-three Massachusetts regiments). The poet John Greenleaf Whittier forsook his pacifism for an hour to get a glimpse of the marching Blacks. It was the only regiment he viewed during the war, and he never forgot the scene. The face of spectator Frederick Douglas was flushed with pride as his two sons, Lewis and Charles, stepped along the line of march, their Enfield rifles swinging to the beat of Patrick Gilmore's martial music.

"On jammed Boston Common the troops (one thousand strong) passed in review before Governor Andrew, the mayor of the city, and Senator Henry Wilson. The eyes of twenty thousand onlookers followed the marching men, who made an excellent appearance. The *Boston Transcript* commented upon 'the general precision attending their evolutions,' and 'their ease and uniformity in going through the manual.'

"In front rode Colonel Shaw, his head erect under his high felt army hat with cord. Young Shaw sat well on a horse, and his mother, Sarah Sturgis Shaw, murmured how blessed she felt as she watched her beloved and only son. Another spectator, the talented seventeen-year-old Negro, Edmonia Lewis, never forgot how handsome he looked; a year later when she sculptured a bust of him she drew heavily from that vivid memory.

"From the scene of the dress parade, the regiment marched to Battery Wharf. En route the band played the John Brown song 'while passing over ground moistened by the blood of Crispus Attucks,' a Negro who was the first patriot to shed his blood in the Revolutionary War.

"One of the soldiers of the Fifty-fourth had just written a poem whose lines remembered Attucks:

O give us a flag, all free without a slave,
We'll fight to defend it as our fathers did so brave.

"Shortly after one o'clock, the regiment boarded *The DeMolay*, readied for her maiden voyage; three hours later, the lines were cut and the steamer eased from her moorings." The Fifty-fourth, their courage and their music had become a part of American military history.

The need of individual slaves to be of value in what they saw as the war that would be the instrument of their freedom was pervasive; it hummed in the collective bosom of the community. Drafted by the mistress into helping hide the plantation valuables, slaves remembered, with the coming of the Union troops, the location of the hiding places.

First tour of Fisk Jubilee Singers.

CHAINS

"No more

slavery chains for me."

"No more slavery chains for me."

George Rawick writes of Black secret fraternal organizations, which "became centers of resistance during the Civil War," and Benjamin Quarles relates the existence of the "Loyal League" in Virginia in Confederate territory, "whose purpose was to speed runaway slaves on their journeys and to furnish information to the Union commanders concerning the movement of the rebels. The Loyal League supplied a courier who took (the) documents through rebel lines to Washington."

Quarles goes on to describe the informal organization of the slave community itself, and how it operated to assist escaping Union soldiers from one spot of safety to the next, as the slaves moved behind Confederate lines to reunite the escapees with Union troops.

Black men, women and children, still in place as plantation slaves courageously assisted, escaped Union prisoners in every manner possible. Excerpts from a diary kept by Lieutenant Hannibal Johnson, Third Marine Infantry, escaping with three other Union officers, corroborates this slave activity. One of his many entries states: "Still in the woods, the women coming to us twice during the day to bring food and inform us that a guide will be ready at dark. God bless the poor slaves... Nov. 25: Lay in the woods all day and at night went to Ford's plantation to get food. Here the Negroes could not do enough for us, supplying us with edibles of nice character... Nov. 28: A guide by the name of Bob (then) a guide by the name of George who hid us in the woods. At dark went to Negro quarters where a nice chicken supper was waiting us."

The men, after successfully completing a slave-aided journey of approximately five weeks and 200 miles, were able to rejoin their Union comrades.

The Civil War found master and slave each consumed by the same urgency: an overwhelming need to be in some way directly involved. The master, eyes bloodshot at even the notion of endangered privilege, determined to stand guard over a Way of Life; the slave, eyes blinded by the notion of Himself as Man, anxious to seize the moment, secure the vision. Both, driven.

Robert Smalls, a slave and a member of the crew of *The Planter*, a Confederate vessel, made plans

to hurry his moment. Sources do not agree as to whether *The Planter* was a gunboat or a transport steamer, nor do they agree as to the number of lives for which Smalls was ultimately responsible. What is beyond dispute is that in the early morning of May 13, 1862, with all three white officers having gone ashore to sleep, the slave Smalls, "in pindrop silence," led his wife, his children and an unverified number of others down into the recesses of *The Planter*, assumed command of the vessel and, resisting a natural urge to hurry, sailed it with great deliberation past Confederate checkpoints while wearing one of the officer's hats, assuming that familiar posture and replying appropriately to the challenges of the Confederate sentries. Once past, and not a moment too soon, he lowered the vessel's Confederate flags, ran a white sheet of truce up the mast, barely avoiding fire from the Union blockade, and crossed from slavery into Union-held waters, and Freedom.

As a result of his daring, Smalls was made the first Black captain in the Union navy; was awarded a large sum for the successful delivery of "booty," in this case an enemy vessel; and during Reconstruction,

was elected representative from South Carolina to the nation's Congress, where he served for six years. His was simply another example of the compulsion to participate, to 'do something,' anything that fell within one's province, a compulsion to play a role in the prospect of Freedom that coursed like an electric charge through the hearts and minds of the Nation's slaves. Small wonder the music of the period was energizing and spiritual and could move the listener to foot-stomping and tears.

Black folks were also creatively involved, to the extent that creators of new verses to familiar tunes abounded. Even Sojourner Truth, ex-slave and abolitionist speaker, was responsible for six verses of a song written to the John Brown tune and entitled "The Valiant Soldier." One of the verses reads:

> *We are done with hoeing cotton,*
> * we are done with hoeing corn*
> *We are colored Yankee soldiers, as sure as you are born.*
> *When Massa hears us shouting,*
> * he will think 'tis Gabriel's horn*
> *As we go marching on.*

When the First Arkansas Volunteers, identified by the letters *C. T.*, for "colored troops" (as were all

Black soldiers by Congressional decree, sang their marching song, "Glory Hallelujah," to the familiar tune of "John Brown's Body," they revised the language. With its new insightful, audacious lyrics, it sounded nothing like Harriet Beecher Stowe's more austere sentiments, usually sung to the same popular melody. The song, its jocular, challenging imagery unmistakable, is guaranteed to "joy the spirit."

"Free at Las'," another spiritual classic, celebrates not only freedom by decree but the concept of internal freedom of spirit, as well as the external freedom that many slaves provided for themselves, their family members and friends throughout the more than 200-year-long winter of slavery, by courageous, inventive and daring escape, or hard-won purchase.

The song's title claimed a permanent place in the annals of the Civil Rights Era and became indelibly imprinted in the hearts and minds of Americans everywhere when it was dramatically delivered as the emotion-packed final line of Dr. Martin Luther King's famous "I Have a Dream" speech during the 1963 March on Washington.

Its jubilee is contagious; the listener cannot help but join in.

$100 REWARD!

RANAWAY

From the undersigned, living on Current River, about twelve miles above Doniphan, Ripley County, Mo., on 2nd of March, 1860, A NEGRO MAN, about 30 years old, weighs about 60 pounds; high forehead, with a scar on it; had on brown pants and coat, very much worn, and an old black wool hat; shoes size No. 11.

The above reward will be given to any person who may apprehend this negro out of the State; and fifty dollars if apprehended in this State outside of Ripley county, or $25 if taken in Ripley county.

APOS TUCKER.

COUNTRY MOODS

C ountry Moods consists of songs largely defined by locale or category. Although they share a common African matrix, performance and content are always creatively singular, influenced by circumstance and the individual involved. Running a gamut of styles and subjects, the stories and scenes offer a perspective on rural Black life after the Civil War. The listener can feast on words and music popular before the turn of the century. Although indigenous to the rural South and shaped by that

"Both **holler** and street cry contribute **essential** elements to the blues."

terrain and that experience, the music and narratives would have traveled naturally with the people as they journeyed away from the South to the cities.

"Run Squirrel, Whoa Mule" offers a glimpse of a classic African cultural device: the challenge to excel creatively in a demonstration of style and skill. In this instance, multi-timing and call and response are the critical elements as the tempo escalates, and antiphonal multi-timing becomes a trope repeated in three of the four children's songs.

In "'Way Go Lily," the children are not above the whimsical fantasy of controlling ol' massa and missis. In "Fox Chase," we hear a master musician, Brownie McGhee, replicate the excitement of hounds in full cry. This example of instrumental expertise was a standard performance piece, and would have been a popular favorite requested again and again. "Grey Goose" is a tale of indomitability, with the goose that can neither be caught nor killed as metaphor for the invincibility and wiliness of an otherwise downtrodden people who have mastered the arts of survival.

There are 'hollers' for the occasions when emotion or distance render ordinary song or voice inadequate. It is important to consider, however, that African languages are tonal to the extent that even drum tones deliver actual words and are thus able to speak so precisely in this or that dialect that they can be understood only if the listener, even if African, understands the specific language or dialect being spoken. That said, the 'holler' that seemed to have been merely a wordless call may easily have been delivering specific information or messages, given its undeniably tonal quality.

The hoedown has a classic 4/4 crossover rhythm, and, finally, there is Belafonte at his sensitive best in the tender "Go to Sleepy."

1896

In *Plessy v. Ferguson*, the U.S. Supreme Court upholds the doctrine of "separate but equal," ushering in the legally sanctioned culture of Jim Crow.

CITY
MOODS

City Moods presents a panorama of Black life in the city, perhaps towards the end of the 19th century. It attempts to suggest not only the sounds of the city, but the sights, colors, smells and events of life in those times, in those places, for those particular people: an ambiance like none other.

George Marek would insist that he has seen the shabby peddler with the colorful hat turning into the bustle of a city street, that he has heard the sound of the plodding horse as it pulls the creaking wagon, piled high with every conceivable kind of fresh foodstuff. The cry of the peddler calling his wares is but a few steps removed from the field holler of his country cousin. Both holler and street cry contribute essential elements to the blues.

Children's games are more rhythmically sophisticated than one would expect, and the blues one hears in a honky-tonk clearly reflect the constriction and abrasiveness of urban life, particularly as experienced in the Black community. A watermelon peddler cajoles prospective clients, his pushcart laden almost beyond his strength. A woman with blackberries to sell is much more astute. She chooses a quiet, tree-shaded street. It is still early; the berries balanced on a large tray on her head must be sold while they retain the moisture of that day's dew. A blind street singer intones the blues. A few streets distant, in more genteel precincts, he will sing the gospel with equal fervor. Listen, now, to the cries of peddlers, the sounds and moods of the city.

Duke Ellington is born. Also that year, Scott Joplin's "Maple Leaf Rag" is published.

Black song, historically, is merely a natural part of life's process for persons of African descent, and transcending travail through music, merely survival movement; an inherent part of the spirit. Black song delights, informs, entertains, and one finds that sadness, irony, nonsense, a clear analysis of adversity and, of course, humor, are but sides of the same coin.

"Let the Deal Go Down" is a clever replication of a card game where fortune and misfortune are each treated with humor and good spirits. "Betty and Dupree" is a ballad reputedly based on a true-life incident. In trying to provide for Betty, daughter of a plantation owner and his forbidden love, Dupree, a free ex-slave commits a robbery. He flees but is caught by police who watch Betty's mail. The authenticity of the story is underscored by the fact that the father of the guitarist in this recording shined shoes outside the scene of Dupree's crime.

BALLADS & FROLICS

"Black song delights, informs, entertains, and one finds…sadness, irony, nonsense, a clear analysis of adversity and, of course, humor…"

JOHN HENRY, THE STEEL DRIVING MAN

John Henry was a railroad man.
  He worked from six 'till five,
"Raise 'em up bullies and let 'em drop down,
  I'll beat you to the bottom or die."

John Henry said to his captain:
  "You are nothing but a common man,
Before that steam drill shall beat me down,
  I'll die with my hammer in my hand."

John Henry said to the Shakers:
  'You must listen to my call,
Before that steam drill shall beat me down,
  I'll jar these mountains till they fall."

John Henry's captain said to him:
  "I believe these mountains are caving in "
John Henry said to his captain: "Oh Lord!"
  "That's my hammer you hear in the wind."

John Henry he said to his captain:
  "Your money is getting mighty slim,'
When I hammer through this old mountain,
  Oh Captain will you walk in?"

John Henry's captain came to him
  With fifty dollars in his hand,
He laid his hand on his shoulder and said:
  "This belongs to a steel driving man."

John Henry was hammering on the right side,
  The big steam drill on the left,
Before that steam drill could beat him down,
  He hammered his fool self to death.

They carried John Henry to the mountains,
  From his shoulder his hammer would ring,
She caught on fire by a little blue blaze
  I believe these old mountains are caving in.

John Henry was lying on his death bed,
  He turned over on his side,
And these were the last words John Henry said
  "Bring me a cool drink of water before I die."

John Henry had a little woman,
  Her name was Pollie Ann,
He hugged and kissed her just before he died,
  Saying, "Pollie, do the very best you can."

John Henry's woman heard he was dead,
  She could not rest on her bed,
She got up at midnight, caught that No. 4 train,
  "I am going where John Henry fell dead."

They carried John Henry to that new burying ground
  His wife all dressed in blue,
She laid her hand on John Henry's cold face,
  "John Henry I've been true to you."

Price 5 Cents   W. T. BLANKENSHIP.

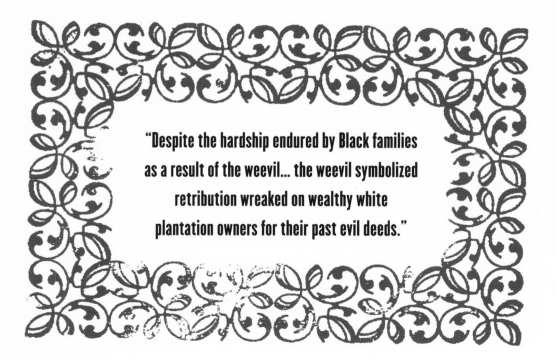

"Despite the hardship endured by Black families as a result of the weevil... the weevil symbolized retribution wreaked on wealthy white plantation owners for their past evil deeds."

James Reese Europe leads the Clef Club Orchestra in an early performance by African Americans at Carnegie Hall.

To be "pimp slick" was to suggest that one had a "back East" or big-city background; to be called "Eas' Man" was to be admired for one's cleverness in living by one's wits. "Eas' Man" may or may not have been a pimp; nevertheless, the song is provocative.

"John Henry" is perhaps the most famous and long-lived of all African American folk-ballads. That he lived seems indisputable, although to this day it excites debate. He is our Black epic hero, doing, as poet Etheridge Knight has written, "things we dreamed of doing but could not." His was the heaviest hammer, the fastest, the baddest drill; and in competition with the new-fangled stream drill, a proud John Henry, committed to his sense of Self, put his manhood on the line and won the all-day contest, triumphing over the stream drill by eighteen inches. Joy was short-lived; he fell dead on the spot, and the deed, so magnificent, so unbelievable, has come down to us as legend. Given the changing face of history, however, the notion that John Henry is merely myth no longer holds. According to new research, a picture of him actually exists.

Harry Belafonte sings the final "Boll Weevil," delineating the devastation wreaked by the scourge that swept up from Mexico after the Civil War, ate its way across whole areas of the South, wiping out entire cotton crops, creating widespread unemployment, and ultimately influencing the migration of desperate Black families to the North and East. Despite the hardship endured by Black families as a result of the weevil, the song owed its popularity to the feeling that the weevil symbolized retribution wreaked on wealthy white plantation owners for their past evil deeds.

Harry T. Burleigh, who had studied with Dvořák, has his *Jubilee Songs of the United States of America*, the first collection of spiritual arrangements, published.

Georege Marek describes Bad Men, Booze and Minstrels as containing a re-creation of an early minstrel show, as well as separate songs that revolve around bad men and the mythology of their crimes, some depicted with humor, others delivered in a blues mode.

The "baddest" of the bad men was surely "Stagolee." According to Marek, there is good evidence that Stagolee lived and was well-known to police in Memphis. However, his reputation far outstripped the possibilities of real life; he is even mentioned in the Louisiana version of the John Henry legend as John Henry's nemesis; and in folklore he comes fairly close to being a stand-in for Satan himself.

Another legendary bad man was Joe Turner, the central figure in "Joe Turner Blues." Turner was a callous sheriff whom Marek credits with institutionalizing the chain-gang system to the point where it rivaled slavery. W. C. Handy reputedly described this song as the first blues he ever heard.

"Honey, Take a Whiff on Me," fairly well-known in many versions, apparently has its origin in the drug culture, although many campers have innocently chanted campfire versions of what appeared to be an innocuous ditty.

The last part of this section is the re-creation of the Minstrel Scene.

MINSTRELS

No movement in American music has had a more profound effect on American popular culture over the life of this nation's history than the minstrel tradition. The precursor to the tent-show traditions, vaudeville, modern American musical theater, and even Tin Pan Alley, minstrel theater's most disturbing element was its fixation on presenting a distortion of Black life. These images persist to this day in all of American media and entertainment.

The minstrel tradition is the adaptation and mutation of plantation songs, or slave songs, into formal entertainment in the theatrical tradition. This became the bedrock of much of the common musical vernacular from the mid-18th century through the early 20th century and beyond. It presented negative characterizations of Black folk as fools, buffoons, liars, lovers of liquor, and given to thievery. This racist distortion of Black life by white minstrels served as one half of what might be seen as the twin fists of white supremacy: *Plessy v. Ferguson* established de jure segregation as the law of the land, and the thrust of the minstrel images, supported by the popular literature of the time, "clarified" for the society contrived and unwarranted beliefs in Black inferiority. Throughout the 19th century, this was America's most popular form of entertainment. It significantly affected the 20th century, and wearing different clothing and using different vernacular still colors the relationships between blacks and whites in the new millennium.

Early on, African Americans had no stages on which to perform except those provided by minstrel theater; Blacks and whites could not share the stage, and Blacks could only perform in roles provided by the owners of minstrel theaters—roles that accommodated the crude expectations of the audience, that is, Black actors, often wearing burnt cork, imitating the white performers who, in blackface, were presenting distorted depictions of 'black life.'

Musicologist Eileen Southern, perhaps the most celebrated scholar of the music of Black Americans, generally divides the minstrel tradition between pre- and post–Civil War and as it was practiced by Blacks and whites. She identifies the tradition from the 1760s to around 1820 as being rather more benign in its approach to Black characterizations, typically depicting the African American as a tragic figure or one to be pitied—in either case, a sympathetic portrayal. The alternate Black personas of minstrelsy were the caricatures of the plantation slave "Jim Crow," dressed in rags, with a thick accent, and that of the urban Black as "Zip Coon," a would-be dandy, whose personality flaws are as endemic as his dress is outlandish. As the adaptations by white entertainers working in blackface veered more towards the direction of comedy, the characterizations become more mean-spirited and disparaging. We have Thomas

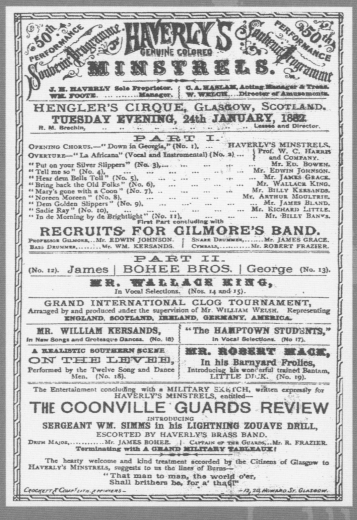

Dartmouth Rice to thank, according to minstrel historian T. Allston Brown, for the creation of the "Jim Crow" character. Supposedly, Rice observed an old, deformed slave stable hand going about his work singing music from the folk tradition of slaves from Kentucky, one chorus of which went as follows:

First on the heel tap, den on de toe
Ebery time I wheel about I jump Jim Crow.

At that point in the song, the slave jumped in the air.

Rice stole the song and the character, added lyrics, costumes and movements in which he further exaggerated the slave's deformity to enhance the comic effect of the act, and published and performed the song in theaters throughout his tours to enormous success, becoming known as "Daddy Rice—the Father of Minstrelsy." Historian Southern credits the Virginia Minstrels with the first minstrel theater production in 1843, and cites numerous examples of successful white minstrel troupes, such as the Christy Minstrels.

There were rare pre–war instances when Blacks, not performing in blackface, appeared with minstrel shows or gained independent recognition as performers. Southern cites such performers as William Henry Lane (*circa* 1825–1852), better known as Master Juba, who gained such worldwide acclaim for his dancing and musicianship that he was described by Charles Dickens as "the greatest dancer known." While entertainers from both races performed what were now known as minstrel or "Ethiopian" songs, the interpretations differed widely. Southern wryly pulls these quotes from an essay by J. Kinnard, which she found in an 1845 issue of *Knickerbocker Magazine*:

> *Who are our true rulers? The Negro poets to be sure. Do they not set the fashion, and give laws to the public taste? Let one of them, in the swamps of Carolina, compose a new song, and it no sooner reaches the ear of a white amateur, than it is written down, amended (that is, almost spoilt), printed and then put upon a course of rapid dissemination, to cease only with the utmost bounds of Anglo Saxondom, perhaps with the world. Meanwhile, the poor author digs away with his hoe, utterly ignorant of his greatness. But our national melodists have many imitators. Half the songs published as theirs are, as far as the words are concerned, the production of "mean whites"; but base counterfeits as they are, they pass current with most people as genuine negro songs. Thus is it ever with true excellence!*

Kinnard goes on to point out that the Black creators of these songs often improvised stanzas as the mood and the environment suited them. It is undeniable, as Southern asserts, and composers like Stephen Foster clearly demonstrate that "the leading figures of the entertainment world spent the better part of the nineteenth century imitating" the culture of the African Americans.

Emancipation and its aftermath saw a great increase in the number of Black entertainers who were now able to join the ranks of minstrel troupes sweeping the country in the latter half of the nineteenth century. Names such as W. C. Handy, "the Father of the Blues," popular song composer James Bland, who wrote "Carry Me Back to Old Virginny," and Gussie Lord Davis, the first Black composer to achieve success in Tin Pan Alley, all started as minstrel musicians. There were even Black businessmen who had their own minstrel companies. The larger, more commercial white-owned minstrel companies traveled by Pullman cars and had parades organized prior to the show in order to drum up business. By this time, the repertoire of the shows had expanded dramatically. Black minstrel shows added spirituals, operatic airs, marches and other material to go with the traditional blend of novelty tunes, ballads and specialties.

The re-creation of a minstrel program that we've included in this anthology is an encapsulated version of a show, minus the derogatory "coon songs"; which would have generally run about an hour and forty-five minutes in its entirety.

Traditionally, the shows required an interlocutor, or master of ceremonies, interacting jocularly with the performers. Minstrel shows were usually divided into three parts: The first was comprised of coon songs and jokes, the second part, or olio, presented specialty and novelty acts, created from the individual skills of various members of the troupe. The third, the walk-around finale, or afterpiece, allowed the central players to move to the front of the stage for final performances, while the remainder of the troupe provided accompaniment from the background, a moment, more often than not, retained in contemporary musical theatre.

According to Allen Woll, writing in *Black Musical Theater: From Coontown to Dreamgirls*, by 1890, "most of the 1,490 Black actors enumerated by the census were employed in touring minstrel companies (but) saddled with the stage conventions of minstrelsy," and despite extraordinary Black talent, competence, and the most diligent, ongoing efforts of Black artists, change occurred gradually, and significant change not until the late 1800s.

With the arrival of the dapper, highly educated, ambitious Johnson brothers, Rosamond and James Weldon, in New York City in 1899; their song-writing collaboration with Bob Cole; their close associations with other resident New York entertainers and musicians; and their resultant influence on white New York publishers, the era of coon songs on Broadway that had resisted Black efforts for so long was about to end. Racism is a stubborn opponent; It would take almost another decade.

—AL PRYOR

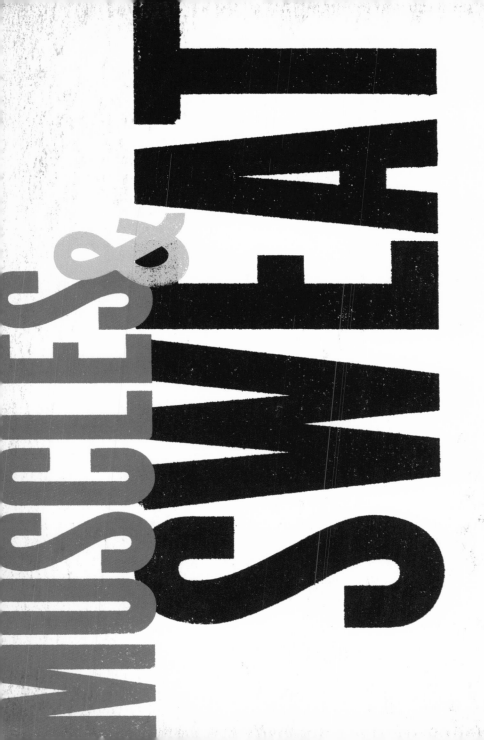

MUSCLES & SWEAT

Africans were captured, enslaved and brought to America for one reason: To work. Their raison d'etre was work; the only justification for their existence was work; their fortunes depended on the quality and quantity of the work they produced, and of no small importance was their ability to second guess the caprice of the callous drivers, cruel overseers or even the profit-driven owners who often found it less costly to replace slaves than to maintain them under humane conditions. Most slave owners worried very little, if at all, about the welfare of slaves, whose definition was not too different from that of cattle. Born, bought and sold to work or to procreate was their destiny, and they died when worn, abused, and mutilated; they were no longer able to work.

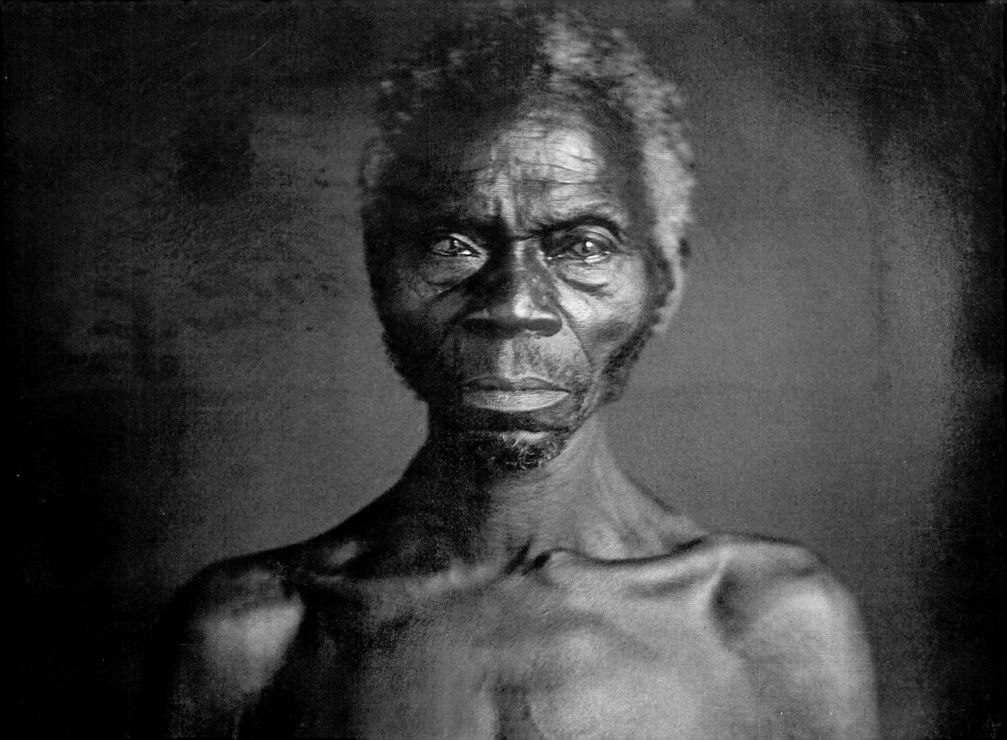

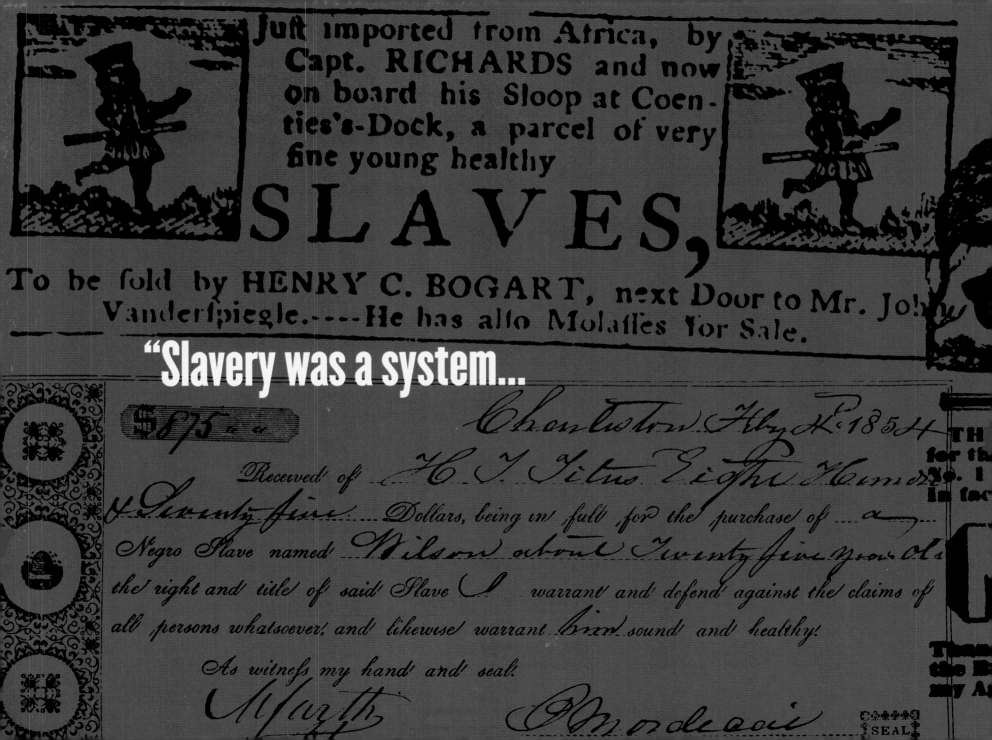

Just imported from Africa, by Capt. RICHARDS and now on board his Sloop at Coenties's-Dock, a parcel of very fine young healthy

SLAVES,

To be sold by HENRY C. BOGART, next Door to Mr. John Vanderspiegle.-----He has also Molasses for Sale.

"Slavery was a system...

"African American work songs are among the most poignant, most moving in the pantheon of Black musics; they sang an indomitable group spirit; quite incredible given the circumstances."

Of course there were exceptions, but for the millions who worked from "can to can't," from first light to way past dark sometimes, the fact that some slaves lived lives somewhat less onerous, was of little satisfaction.

The manner in which captive African men, women and children were turned into "slaves," and the ways communities of slaves and their descendants, and their descendants were brought into being and continued in bondage varied from city to farm, from state to state, from mistress to mistress, from owner/businessman to the poor white entrepreneur who owned one unfortunate Negro woman. Slavery was a system, a brutal, dehumanizing engine that drove the economy of the South, and ensured, for the more fortunate white Southerner, a certain quality of life.

The slaves' best efforts to avoid the caprice of cruel masters, mistresses, overseers and drivers were never enough to ensure that they, their loved ones or their friends survived unscarred, unscathed. They existed to work; they were battered because they existed; yet, against all logic, they sang. The music went on; their creative approach to life went on.

Their African-matrixed cultural infrastructure was so present, so strong, so integral a part of their being that, empowered by it, they could transcend physical pain and emotional trauma and create music that left a permanent record of their superior human capacity for nobility under duress. This collection provides contemporary listeners with some sense of that.

At the end of the Civil War, in the wake of the departing victorious Northern army, the South, crushed and humiliated in defeat, began to count its losses: Foremost, its dead sons, husbands and brothers—over a hundred thousand of them under the age of seventeen (for a nation always sends its brightest, bravest youth to that initial sacrifice)—its women and children emerging from secret places on pillaged farms; many of its cities destroyed; Sherman's march to the sea, an obscenity in Southern eyes; food in scant supply; crops nonexistent and its store of livestock decimated.

Within that frame of devastation and want, the South fed its will to live again, its need to rebuild and to regain its former sense of self and privilege on the streams of hate and resentment that predictably flowed through its veins.

Yankees, white carpetbaggers and suspected Union sympathizers were its natural focus, but Black men, women and children experienced the brunt of Southern rage, and a very real, brutal, undeclared war of revenge and retribution took place despite the presence of Federal administrators from the North and, often, in the very face of Federal troops who were sent to monitor post-war behavior. The newly freed slaves, reveling in their unbelievable release from bondage, were very natural targets for lynchings, burnings and beatings, all of which became mere spectator sport.

Eubie Blake and Noble Sissl's *Shuffle Along* opens on Broadway. The first Black record company, Black Swan Records, is founded. The Baptist National Convention publishes *Gospel Pearls*.

Although, in time, Reconstruction worked to introduce a drastic change in lifestyle for both Black and white Southerners, any real notion of release from external control was a long time coming for Blacks, despite the new "freedom." They were, in the main, without jobs, homes, tools, money, food or means of transportation, and there was little historical reason to trust white Southerners, whose fortunes were only a little better than those of the new freedmen. Despite

all this, Black folk pooled pennies, created makeshift schools and, in time, would initiate a system of free public education for all. And they sang; always the music.

In time, the South would recover, Blacks would move into politics, go on to control several Southern state legislatures, and even enter the Congress of the United States as legislators. The backlash, however, would be swift and devastating, as the South, still nursing venom, welcomed the formation of secret organizations dedicated to reinstituting all of the ramifications of white power; and a reign of terror ensued. Blacks, regardless of gender or age, were brutalized, their property confiscated, their small businesses burned, and peonage reinstituted.

Free Black men were often charged with non-existent crimes and illegally jailed. At a time when even idleness was defined as a crime, the commission of a crime was not requisite. Forced to provide what became a reservoir of free labor, they were assigned to 'chain gangs,' that is, to work outdoors, chained together, and often to sleep together huddled in metal cages.

Living conditions and treatment were not very different from those in the infamous Nazi work camps;

Black life was absolutely without value. Lands needed to be cleared, roads were being built, and across the country, an elaborate transportation system was being established—possibly an initial public foray into privatization, for the prisoners' labor could be privately contracted. If so, "They were transported in horse-drawn cages between worksites where they also slept at night. The cages were usually seven to eight feet in width and eighteen feet long. Eighteen men were typically bunked in the cage with a night bucket, a pail of drinking water and a stove. Most remained chained at night (and), as any movement would rattle the chains, the prisoner would have to yell out 'Gettin'up!' to the guard to receive permission before using the bucket. The wagons were covered with tarpaulins in bad weather, and prisoners were likely to remain in the cages from noon Saturday until work resumed on Monday morning. Every meal was the same: A square of corn pone, three slices of fried pig fat and a dose of sorghum," according to the *Encyclopedia of American Prisons*.

Although conscripted into chain gangs, the men tried to make their labor less onerous by singing songs such as "Ho Boys, Cancha Line 'Em?"

A work song is any song that moves the work along faster and makes its monotony and drudgery a little easier to bear. They are often ordinary songs in which the words have nothing to do with the work being done, but the rhythmic pulse of the music accents the physical demands of the task at hand. There are also those pieces whose lyrics relate solely to the task at hand, or can be adjusted to do so. These are clearly work songs, but with a range of utility limited to the object of their words. This program contains examples of both types, starting with "Ho Boys, Cancha Line 'Em?," a rail-lining song. The men use long bars to wedge the rails into alignment for new spikes. In "Good Ir'n," we hear a straw boss, in this instance Harry Belafonte, using a combination of goad and lead to accomplish the unpleasant task of stacking rails along a right-of-way.

These are followed by "Go on, Ol' Gator" and two wood-chopping songs made popular by prisoners. According to Marek, the chain gang owed its beginnings, in Tennessee, to the military governor sent to administer Nashville during Reconstruction.

Thoughts of 'mother' and home, as sung in the nostalgic and poignant "Doncha Hear Yo' Po' Mother

Build Thee More Stately Mansions by Aaron Douglas

Callin'?" are common to men out of circulation for long periods. The last two songs in this section are the "River Sounding Chant," which re-creates the romantic sounds along the river as conceived by Mark Twain, and "Nobody's Business, Lord, But Mine," another piquant, all-purpose song in a blues mode, used in this instance by a gang of gravel tampers engaged in road construction.

George Marek believes that Joe Turner, a callous Southern sheriff, can be credited with having invented new ways of heightening the horror and brutality of the chain gang. An additional observation is that suppressing or containing the hapless is hardly an individual invention; chains have been the hallmark of oppression, have spoken the language of confinement since man first decided to place others under control in ways that seriously altered the quality of their lives. While the practice has abated in America, it has not ceased. As late as 1997, Arizona's Maricopa County sheriff, Joe Arpaio, assigned women prisoners to work on chain gangs.

What is noteworthy is that, despite the traumatic experience of serving what often became indefinite periods of months or years on the chain gang, the prisoners produced a power-filled music pulsed by a group determination to survive; a music that nudged the men on through long hours of backbreaking labor in the sun or water, under the guns of brutish guards.

African American work songs are among the most poignant, most moving in the pantheon of Black musics; they sing an indomitable group spirit, quite incredible, given the circumstances.

MY GOD IS A ROCK

A frican-matrixed art, whether presented through song, worship, or dance is functional in the telling of tales and fables, the creation of makeshift toys for the children, or the crafting of musical instruments. The slaves' search for surcease, for emotional release from trial and trauma, was ongoing, an integral part of the slave community's efforts to survive as whole human beings.

Dr. Martin Luther King, Jr. waves to a crowd at a demonstration to protest racial inequality, Lincoln Memorial, Washington, D.C., August 28, 1963.

"My God Is a Rock" is an unequivocal statement of the slave's faith in a redemptive power greater than him or herself; as an absolute, an ongoing expression of confidence. God was accessible, approachable, all-powerful, and the slave, male or female, however brutalized and downtrodden, would survive.

Howard Thurman calls "We Are Climbin' Jacob's Ladder" the great pilgrim spiritual. Given the overriding sense of 'salvation tomorrow' that fueled the inner-life of the slave, Thurman suggests that, implicit in the ladder imagery of the song, is the sense of a goal and the certainty that each person must face the figure—undoubtedly God—at the top of the ladder. This spiritual occupies a special place in the canon of spirituals, and it is as moving an experience sung at the beginning of the new millennium as it must have been when it encouraged a weary slave community to "keep on keeping on" in the face of overwhelming odds.

The excerpt from one of Dr. King's speeches is set for posterity against the exquisite harmonic structure of a de Paur arrangement. This is followed by a final triumphant statement of struggle, of victory, and of Freedom claimed.

"God was accessible, approachable, all-powerful, and the slave, male or female, however brutalized and downtrodden, would survive."

What we may have come to understand as we have opened, not merely to an appreciation of the music in this extraordinary collection but possibly to a new perspective of the sociopolitical climate of the times as well, may be that our original proposition regarding the relationship of creativity to experience, has value;

That as a result of being enslaved, Africans found themselves in a Manichaean struggle: The empirical contest that the peoples of the world wage for humankind's divine right to exploit Original Privilege (e.g., to live in basic relationship to the forces of good even when seemingly overwhelmed by the forces of evil);

That if, in our interior, our inner-selves, we understand Original Privilege as a given, and the captives did, they also understood the value, indeed, the power, of the spoken word, and therefore we may further understand;

"From Spirituals to Swing" concert held at Carnegie Hall.

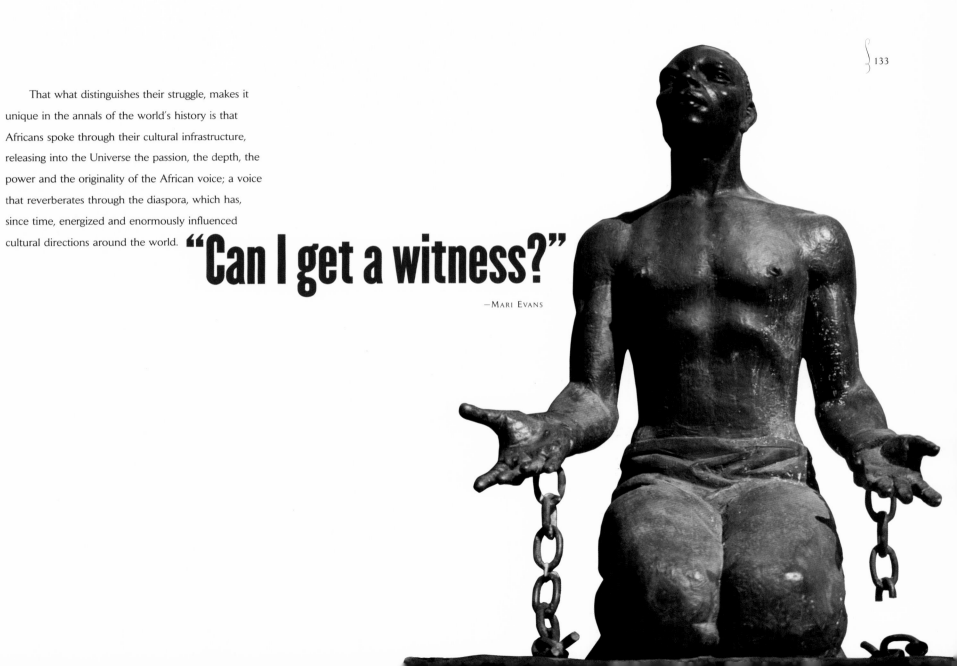

That what distinguishes their struggle, makes it unique in the annals of the world's history is that Africans spoke through their cultural infrastructure, releasing into the Universe the passion, the depth, the power and the originality of the African voice; a voice that reverberates through the diaspora, which has, since time, energized and enormously influenced cultural directions around the world. **"Can I get a witness?"**

—MARI EVANS

CHARLES WHITE

Good Night Irene, by the late Charles Wilbert White (1918–1979), is the painting that graces the cover of *The Long Road to Freedom: An Anthology of Black Music*. White is best known for his charcoal drawings, although he is also celebrated for his work as an easel and mural painter, and printmaker. A product of the Art Institute of Chicago, where he studied on scholarship; the Art Students League in New York; and the Taller de Gráfica Popular, in Mexico, where he came under the tutelage of the master Diego Rivera, White would eventually create a number of murals under the auspices of the WPA (Works Project Administration). White worked as an artist in residence at Howard University and served on the faculties of South Side Community Arts Center, the George Washington Carver School and the Otis Art Institute (now the Parson's School of Design).

Critics and art historians argue that Charles White's love of draftsmanship and his interest in the German artist Kathe Kollwitz influenced White's decision to do a great deal of his own work in black and white. However, Harry Belafonte, in whose personal collection this painting is held, points out that, at some point during White's career, he became allergic to ingredients in the paints he was using for his works in color, and that this hastened the move towards charcoal drawings. Of course, the title of the painting that adorns the cover of this box set is an obvious reference to Leadbelly (Huddie Ledbetter, 1888–1949), who popularized the tune "Good Night Irene" in the early 1900s. Leadbelly had a vast repertoire of material culled from early blues, shouts, work songs, spirituals and plantation songs (which formed the backbone of minstrel traditions)—some of the very material included in this anthology.

Originally, Charles White created some drawings specifically for this collection. Belafonte had worked with White before, often including White's work in the set designs of the television shows he produced. When the material contained herein remained unreleased, the works were returned to the artist. Charles White's murals were created for Hampton Institute, the Chicago Public Library and the Mary McLeod Bethune Library. His works are held in the permanent collections of the Library of Congress, Howard University, Syracuse University, the Metropolitan Museum of Art, the Whitney Museum of American Art, the Newark Museum, the Los Angeles County Museum of Art and the Santa Barbara Museum of Art.

LEONARD de PAUR

The great creative force of a real artist is to make something live. Leonard de Paur, who served as the arranger, musical director, researcher and conductor for the performances in this anthology, has done just that.

From its inception, this anthology was destined to be a work of spectacular and immense proportion. Leonard de Paur meticulously researched the music from Africa, the British, French and Dutch West Indies, the Out Islands of North Carolina and Georgia and the influences of the colonies of the United States. Then he carefully selected singers and musicians who would provide accurate readings with the necessary pathos—tender or jocular, bold or serene—who would complement and enhance the tremendous artistry of Mr. Belafonte.

Leonard de Paur (1914–1998) played a central role in the 20th-century music scene and had an extensive career as a conductor and arranger. He worked with Leontyne Price, Odetta, Brock Peters, Shirley Verret and many others, in addition to Harry Belafonte. He appeared as a regular and guest conductor with many symphonies and operas, including the premier of *A Bayou Legend* (William Grant Still), and Broadway musicals such as *Purlie* and *Hallelujah Baby*. He also served as the choral director for classic recordings, including the 1947 opera *Four Saints in Three Acts,* composed by Virgil Thompson.

Born in Summit, New Jersey, de Paur began his career on the vaudeville circuit and soon appeared as a featured soloist at the Capital Theater in New York City. He went on to work as the associate conductor of the Hall Johnson Choir, from 1932 to 1940. In 1936, he became the Director of Music for the New York City Negro Unit of the Federal Theatre, and directed the music for productions such as *Macbeth, Androcles and the Lion, Dr. Faustus, Conjure Man Dies* and *Natural Man*. He composed the music for *Haiti* (William Du Bois) and *S.S. Glencairn* (Eugene O'Neill), and was the musical director of *John Henry,* which starred Paul Robeson, in 1940.

Impressive as that list of accomplishments is, de Paur is most well known for two things: the world renown Infantry Chorus and his pioneering work at Lincoln Center, where he built community outreach programs, such as the tremendously popular Out of Doors program.

During WWII, de Paur served as the choral director for Moss Hart's production of *Winged Victory* for the Army Air Force. Then, assigned to the 372 Infantry Regiment of the Army, Captain de Paur was invited to conduct what became The Infantry Chorus. From 1944 until the end of the war, the chorus sang for war-bond rallies and on radio shows. In 1945, they sang for the inauguration of President Roosevelt. The men toured army, navy and marine installations throughout the Pacific, and eventually moved to the European Theatre to entertain the Occupation Forces.

The Infantry Chorus, managed by Columbia Artists, became one of the leading choral groups in the United States and throughout the world. After the war, with many of the original singers still in the ranks, the chorus became the de Paur Infantry Chorus. For more than fifteen years the group delighted audiences wherever it performed, and developed into successive choruses conducted by de Paur until 1968.

Probably de Paur's greatest contribution to 20th-century music was the dignity and skill with which his groups sang the music of African Americans. In addition, de Paur also integrated concert halls across the country; he always had a clause in his contract stating clearly that all performances would be to integrated audiences.

In 1970, de Paur became the Associate Director of the International Choral Festival, which brought choral groups from 54 countries to Lincoln Center. In 1972, he was appointed Director of Community Affairs for the center where, for the next 16 years, he continued his mission of bringing music to the people.

After more than six decades of conducting and arranging, de Paur stands out as one of the giants of contemporary American music and culture who devoted his life to bringing music to his audiences. In this anthology, he takes the experience and dignity of a race of people whose music has sustained them on all of their journeys and—with its sadness and mirth, levity and desperation—makes the music personal for listeners of any generation.

—J. HAMILTON GRANDISON
MARCH 5, 2001

Photographer Roy DeCarava (born 1919) is beloved in the jazz community for his extraordinary portraits of great jazz artists, such as his famous double-exposure shot of John Coltrane. DeCarava is another example of a talented fellow African American artist whose work Harry Belafonte has showcased. DeCarava's photographs provide us with the only visual record we have of the original sessions for this anthology. A product of Cooper Union, the WPA Harlem Arts Center and the Carver Art School in New York, DeCarava's contributions include having been the first African American to receive a Guggenheim Award in photography, a collaboration with Langston Hughes called *The Sweet Flypaper of Life*, and, in 1954, pioneering the opening of his own photographic gallery, which is generally acknowledged to have been one of the first to proffer the exhibition and sale of photography as fine art. DeCarava's work has been exhibited at the Whitney Museum of American Art, the Museum of Modern Art in New York and the Corcoran Gallery in Washington, D.C.

EXECUTIVE PRODUCERS:
Harry Belafonte and David Belafonte
for Belafonte Enterprises Incorporated, and
Alex Miller for Buddha Records/BMG

PRODUCED BY:
Harry Belafonte, David Belafonte,
Albert C. Pryor and Leonard de Paur

MUSICAL DIRECTION AND ARRANGEMENTS:
Leonard de Paur

ORIGINAL A&R:
Harry Belafonte, Leonard de Paur,
George Marek, Andy Wiswell and others

ORIGINAL TRACKS ENGINEERED BY:
Bob Simson, Ernie Oelrich and others

SOUND RESTORATION, MIXING AND MASTERING:
Michael O. Drexler

ART DIRECTION AND DESIGN:
Carol Bobolts, Jaime Boyle and Deb Schuler/
Red Herring Design

PRODUCTION AND PACKAGING DIRECTOR:
Lou Vaccarelli at BMG, with generous assistance
from International Paper

PHOTO RESEARCH:
Anne Kerman

LINER NOTES:
Mari Evans

ADDITIONAL RESEARCH, TECHNICAL
& EDITING SUPPORT:
Derek R. Phemster, Regina Turner Barclay,
Marie T. Wright, Judy Tharp, Sharon Belle

ADDITIONAL TEXT:
Albert C. Pryor

PROOFREADING AND ADDITIONAL SUPPORT:
Rebecca Salazar

PROJECT COORDINATION FOR B.E.I.:
Albert C. Pryor, with assistance from
Norman Riley

PROJECT COORDINATION FOR BMG:
Mandana Eidgah, Eric Hodge, Jeremy Holiday,
John Hudson, Dana Renert, Rob Santos,
Frank Ursoleo and Traci Werbel

TAPE SUPERVISOR:
Glenn Korman, director, BMG Archives

BMG ARCHIVES RESEARCH STAFF:
Vince Giordano and especially Chick Crumpacker,
whose tireless efforts helped identify many of
the original work tapes

DVD PRODUCER/DIRECTOR:
Gil Gilbert

DVD PRODUCTION COORDINATOR:
Owen Grover

SPECIAL THANKS:
Mrs. Coretta Scott King and the Martin
Luther King Estate, Mrs. Leonard de Paur
and the Leonard de Paur Estate, and the
Charles White Estate for their generous
cooperation with the producers

SPECIAL THANKS ALSO TO:
Howard Dodson, Roberta Yancy, Mary Yearwood,
James Huffman, Antony Toussaint and the staff of the
Schomburg Center for Research in Black Culture
for their work, not only on this anthology, but in the
preservation of African American Culture. Tom Lisanti
at the The New York Public Library, Sandy Lawson
and the Photo Duplication Service at the The Library
of Congress, Dr. Eileen Southern and
Professor Southern, and Wilhelmina Roberts Wynn

THANKS ALSO TO:
Dr. Nii O. Quarcoopome, Scott Hankins and the
staff at the Newark Museum for their help in African
authentication and editorial support, Dave Roberts and
Mark of the Unicorn and special thanks to Murphy

THANKS FROM THE PRODUCERS
TO B.E.I. ASSOCIATES AND AFFILIATES:
John Simson Esq., Michael D. Remer Esq.,
Stu Cantor, Cheryl Pierce and J. Hamilton Grandison

THANKS ALSO TO:
Buddha and BMG staff and their affiliates:
Rick Bleiweiss, Rick Cohen, Seth Cohen,
Laura Dorson, Wolfgang Eckart, Keith Estabrook,
Bob Garbarini, Marc Garrett, Felicia Gearhart,
Joseph Gorman, Dean Harmeyer, Evan Harrison,
Konrad Hilbers, Bob Jamieson, Mike Jason, Pete Jones
and the BMG branch offices, Stephanie Kika,
Marilyn Laverty, Barry LeVine, Jennifer Link, Bill Mauer,
Jim McDermott, Roger Menz, Mike Mjehovich, Bob Morelli,
Gary Newman, Brooke Nochomson, Tom O'Flynn,
Larry Parra, Mindy Pickard, Brian Piperno,
Juliana Plotkin, Joelle Quinn, Scott Richman,
Pamela Robinson, Jason Rosenfeld, Klaus Schmalenbach,
Rolf Schmidt-Holtz, Bill Stafford, Thomas Stein,
Michael Terry, Rick Wilcoxen, and Ola Wirenstrand

SPECIAL THANKS TO RCA VICTOR GROUP: *David Weyner,*
Steve Orselet, Greg Barbero, Stacey Bain, Susan Rosenberg,
Ann Vikstrom, Kathy Callahan

www.BuddhaRecords.com/BlackAnthology
© 2001 Belafonte Enterprises Inc. 74465-99756-2 Printed in U.S.A.

PICTURE CREDITS

COVER PAINTING: *Good Night Irene* by Charles White: Courtesy of the Estate of Charles White PAGE 3 *Bass Concerto* Drawing by Charles White: Courtesy of the Estate of Charles White PAGE 10 *J'Accuse #9* Drawing by Charles White: Courtesy of the Estate of Charles White PAGE 13 *J'Accuse #1* Drawing by Charles White: Courtesy of the Estate of Charles White PAGE 15 *J'Accuse #2* Drawing by Charles White: Courtesy of the Estate of Charles White PAGE 16 *J'Accuse #3* Drawing by Charles White: Courtesy of the Estate of Charles White PAGE 27 Harry Belafonte and George Marek, courtesy of BMG Archives PAGE 28 Gloria Lynne Photograph by Roy Decarava PAGE 29 West African drummers Photograph by Roy DeCarava PAGE 30 Members of the women's chorus ensemble Photograph by Roy DeCarava PAGE 31 Joe WIlliams Photograph by Roy DeCarava PAGES 32-33 Leonard de Paur with members of the children's chorus Photograph by Roy DeCarava PAGE 34 Erzalene Jenkins Photograph by Roy DeCarava PAGE 35 Leonard de Paur directing members of the chorus in rehearsal prior to taping with Harry Belafonte Photograph by Roy DeCarava PAGE 36 Harry Belafonte, Courtesy of BMG Archives PAGE 37 Sonny Terry and Brownie McGhee: Ghetty Images\Archive Photos PAGE 38 Members of the men's choral ensemble with an unidentified vocalist in the foreground Photograph by Roy DeCarava PAGE 39 Dr. Martin Luther King, Jr. with Harry Belafonte, courtesy of Harry Belafonte PAGE 40 Leonard de Paur, Joe Williams and Harry Belafonte Roy DeCarava PAGE 41 West African drummers and students Photograph by Roy DeCarava PAGE 42 West African drummers and students with Harry Belafonte Photograph by Roy DeCarava PAGE 44 OVER LEAF: *Returning from the Cotton Fields in South Carolina,* c. 1860, stereograph by Barnard, negative # 47843: © Collection of The New York Historical Society PAGE 46 *A Slave Gang in Zanzibar:* © Stock Montage PAGE 49 Scars on the back of an escaped slave, Louisiana, 1863: AKG Berlin/SuperStock PAGE 52 Detail from Slave Ship: Photographs and Prints Division, Schomburg Center for Research in Black Culture, The New York Public Library, Astor, Lenox and Tilden Foundations PAGE 53 Kneeling slaves, detail from commemorative plate: Schomburg Center for Research in Black Culture, The New York Public Library, Astor, Lenox and Tilden Foundations PAGE 54 Portrait of Huddie Ledbetter, "Leadbelly": © Bettmann/CORBIS PAGE 55 Map of Africa, c. 1700: Post Museum, Berlin/A.K.G. Berlin/SuperStock PAGE 56 125th Street, looking east from 8th Avenue: Getty Images Hulton|Archive PAGE 62 D'Mba Mask, Simo Society, Baga People, Guini, West Africa, 20th century: Courtesy of the Newark Museum, Gift of Ruth Wilner, 2000.42 PAGE 62 Primitive Yoruba Beaded Container and Cover: Christie's Images/SuperStock PAGES 62–63 Primitive Yoruba Drum for Ifa Ijebu area: Christie's Images/SuperStock PAGE 63 Toy Fishing Boat, Fante people, Ghana, West Africa, 20th Century Purchase 1992, The Members Fund. The Newark Museum, 92.235 PAGE 63 A King's Crown, Yoruba people, Nigeria, West Africa, 20th Century, The Newark Museum, Gift of Ruth Wilner, 2000.43 PAGE 65 Funeral in Virginia: Getty Images-Hulton|Archive-American Stock PAGES 66-67 Detail from Akunitam or "Cloth of the Great," Akan people, Ghana, West Africa, 20th Century Purchase 1986, The Members' Fund, The Newark Museum, 86.238 PAGE 69 Harriet Tubman: Culver Pictures Inc/SuperStock PAGE 73 *The Old Plantation,* artist unknown: Colonial Williamsburg Foundation Abby Aldrich Rockefeller Folk Art Museum, Williamsburg, VA. PAGE 74 African Americans at prayer meeting, 1862: Getty Images-Hulton|Archive-Kean Collection PAGE 77 OVER LEAF: *After the Sale,* market scene in Richmond, VA, by Eyre Crowe: SuperStock PAGES 80-81 *The Bamboula:* Century Magazine General Research Division, The New York Public Library, Astor, Lenox and Tilden Foundations PAGE 87 Enslaved African Americans Escaping: *The Underground Railroad* by William Still Photographs and Prints Division, Schomburg

Center for Research in Black Culture, The New York Public Library, Astor, Lenox and Tilden Foundations PAGE 90 Abraham F. Brown Unidentified photographer (Seated) 54th Massachusetts Infantry Regiment. Tintype, c.1863. MHS # 251: Courtesy of the Massachusetts Historical Society. PAGE 91 William J. Netson Unidentified photographer 54th Massachusetts Infantry Regiment, Tintype, 1863, MHS # 254: Courtesy of the Massachusetts Historical Society PAGE 92 Poster recruiting Black men to fight: Getty Images Hulton|Archive-Kean Collection PAGE 93 "Now in Camp at Readville!" 54th Regiment...: broadside, 1863. MHS # 47: Courtesy of the Massachusetts Historical Society PAGES 95-96 OVER LEAF Slave Tags: Courtesy of the Charleston Museum PAGES 98-99 Portrait of African American Civil War Soldiers c. 1860s: Photographs and Prints Division, Schomburg Center for Research in Black Culture, The New York Public Library, Astor, Lenox and Tilden Foundations PAGE 101 Reward Ad for Runaway: Library of Congress #LC-USZ62-39380 PAGE 103 African American Children Playing Singing Games, Eatonville, Florida 1935: Library of Congress, Prints and Photographs Division Lomax Collection #LC-USZ6-1723 PAGE 104 *Little Boy with Rooster,* by Samuel Roberts Wynn: Courtesy of Wilhelmina Roberts Wynn, Bruccoli Clark Layman Inc. PAGE 105 OVER LEAF: A blackberry party on the road: Getty Images-Hulton|Archive-Lightfoot PAGES 108-109 market scene, Library of Congress #LC-USZ62-122102 PAGE 113 Broadside of *John Henry, The Steel Driving Man,* Attributed to W.T. Blankenship: Courtesy of University of North Carolina at Chapel Hill, Manuscripts Department PAGE 113 John Henry Sculpture at Talcott, West Virginia: Courtesy of Carla Leslie, Summers County Convention and Visitors Bureau PAGE 116 Men Playing Cards: Getty Images-Hulton|Archive PAGE 119 Playbill for Haverly's Minstrels: Courtesy of Dr. Eileen Southern, author of *Music of Black Americans: A History,* With permission to reprint from W.W. Norton PAGE 120 Hymm of the Freedman Poster: Courtesy of Dr. Eileen Southern, author of *Music of Black Americans: A History,* With permission to reprint from W.W. Norton PAGE 121 Sprague's Georgia Minstrels Poster: Harvard Theater Collection, The Houghton Library PAGE 123 Portrait of slave named Renty, The Peabody Museum Harvard University PAGE 124 **(Top)** Advertisement for newly imported African Slaves, **(Bottom)** Receipt for purchase of Wilson, an enslaved man in the amount of $875, Charleston, South Carolina February 4, 1854: Photographs and Prints Division, Schomburg Center for Research in Black Culture, The New York Public Library, Astor, Lenox and Tilden Foundations PAGE 125 **(Left)** Advertisement by slave trader for the purchase of slaves for the New Orleans market, Lexington, Kentucky, July 2, 1853 **(Right)** Credit sale of a choice gang of 41 slaves, Banks' Arcade, Magazine Street New Orleans, February 5, 1856 Photographs and Prints Division, Schomburg Center for Research in Black Culture, The New York Public Library, Astor, Lenox and Tilden Foundations PAGE 126 Southern Railroad Section Gang: Getty Images-Hulton|Archive-Gabriel Hackett PAGE 128 Open Shackle (Detail): Courtesy of Moorland-Springarn Research Center PAGE 129 *Build Thee More Stately Mansions* by Aaron Douglas, 1944 Oil on canvas, 54"x42", Fisk University Galleries, Nashville, Tennessee PAGE 131 Religious Services, *Harper's Weekly,* July 5, 1879, Photographs and Prints Division, Schomburg Center for Research in Black Culture, The New York Public Library, Astor, Lenox and Tilden Foundations PAGE 132 Dr. Martin Luther King, Jr. waves to a crowd at a demonstration to protest racial inequality, Lincoln Memorial, Washington, D.C., August 28, 1963: Getty Images-Hulton|Archive-CNP PAGE 133 Statue Commemorating Abolition: © Macduff Everton/CORBIS PAGES 139-140 OVER LEAF: Kneeling Slaves, Detail from commemorative plate: Photographs and Prints Division, Schomburg Center for Research in Black Culture, The New York Public Library Astor, Lenox and Tilden Foundations.

VISION.
INNOVATION.
TECHNOLOGY.
IMAGINATION.
*EXPERIENCE...*INTERNATIONAL PAPER

International Paper is proud to be the official sponsor of the packaging for *The Long Road To Freedom: An Anthology of Black Music.*

International Paper worked hard to capture the spiritual impact of the music and Harry Belafonte's vision for the anthology. As the world's largest paper, packaging and forest products company, we pooled our resources to make this customized box set truly unique. Combining old-style gravure printing with modern techniques such as offset lithography, stamping and embossing as well as fabric imported from Europe, this presentation reflects the historical events and cultural dynamics of the African experience in America.

The packaging, which includes a tri-fold multi-CD collector's box and accompanying case-bound book, was designed with great care to ensure quality and longevity. The book uses several International Paper fine papers.

We hope that you enjoy the experience of *The Long Road to Freedom: An Anthology of Black Music* as much as we have.

SPECIAL THANKS TO THE FOLLOWING:

SHOREWOOD PACKAGING CORPORATION.
A BUSINESS OF INTERNATIONAL PAPER FOR:

PACKAGE DEVELOPMENT:
> *Duncan Watson and Gary Lenkeit*

COORDINATION:
> *Anita Samet and Tom Yerves*

PRODUCTION AT THE FOLLOWING FACILITIES:
> Harrison, NJ - *electronic pre-press* Edison, NJ – *outside box cover and text pages using offset lithography*
> Englewood, NJ – *text pages utilizing sheet-fed gravure*
> Waterbury, CT – *manufacture and assembly of box set, book cover and CD package*

CREDITS FOR MATERIALS:

OUTSIDE BOX COVER:
> *Permalin Products' Iris Offset fabric* New York, NY

BOOK COVER:
> *Ecological Fibers*

TRI-FOLD CD PACKAGE. BOOK SPINE AND BOX BASE:
> *Rexam DSI's Siltouch Thermo* South Hadley, MA

BOOK PAPERS:
> *100# Influence dull text*
> *100# Via text*
> *80# Via text*
> *all from International Paper,* Stamford, CT
> *Chartham 30# translucent*

BOOK BINDERY:
> *The Riverside Group* Rochester, NY

National Underground Railroad Freedom Center

Harry Belafonte and The Long Road to Freedom: An Anthology of Black Music are proud to be associated with The National Underground Railroad Freedom Center.

The National Underground Railroad Freedom Center will open in early 2004. It will be built on the northern bank of the Ohio River in Cincinnati as the centerpiece of a $2 billion riverfront development initiative. The Freedom Center will prepare modern-day freedom conductors for action today. Its programs and exhibits will use the values of the Underground Railroad—courage, cooperation and perseverance—to teach how the quest for freedom is relevant today. Visitors will experience state-of-the-art exhibitions, dialogues and collaborative learning, freedom stations and the public Web site. Additional information about the $110 million Freedom Center project can be obtained at 1.877.648.4838, or at www.undergroundrailroad.org.

Continue the Journey

"I'll never turn back no mo."